British Tennis:

Game, Set & ... MESS!

Steve Kitcher

co-author Colin Thorne

2QT Limited (Publishing)

First Edition published 2014 by
2QT Limited (Publishing)
Lancaster LA2 8RE, United Kingdom

Author disclaimer

The opinions expressed in this book are those of the authors. References
to documents, web sites and other journals, newspapers and magazines,
are deemed by the author to be correct at time of writing. Recognition
and understanding of the events and individuals mentioned are in no way
intended to mislead or offend and any facts / figures or comments stated are
based on research the Author has carried out with honest intentions. Every
effort has been made by the author to acknowledge and gain any permission
from organisations and persons mentioned in this book.

Publisher disclaimer

The Publisher does not hold responsibility for any inaccuracies of
information or opinions expressed by the author. At all times editorial
control has remained with the author. As such any enquiries should be
directed to the author.

Cover Design by Hilary Pitt
Illustrations by: Shutterstock.com
Printed by Berforts Information Press Limited

A CIP catalogue record for this book is available
from the British Library
ISBN 978-1-910077-26-9

Contents

FOREWORD

Stephen Debenham

(Tennis Writer for the *Lawn Tennis Writers' Association* and *Tennis Today* magazine)

When Dale Carnegie wrote *How to Win Friends and Influence People*, and Sam Snead launched his ultimate guide called *How to Play Winning Golf*, psychologists and sportsmen paid immediate attention. Every now and then, in all walks of life, someone emerges with a radical approach to his chosen subject – and very often in defiance of the establishment view of that time.

Steve Kitcher, in this simple yet absorbing work, tackles the shortcomings of tennis in Britain whilst also offering his own ideas and solutions, which those running the game have happily ignored for years. This study, reinforced by Steve's long experience as a player and coach, deserves to be dissected by all those who care about the game and might well become a classic reference in years to come.

FROM THE AUTHOR

Now that I am semi-retired and no longer run a tennis academy in the park, I have finally been able to put in writing my thoughts on the mess that has existed in British tennis for far too long – thoughts that have only taken shape because of my very different route into tennis coaching.

In simple and stark terms, why is it that we produce hardly any world-class players?

The answer, as well as the solution, is in this book.

I may be rocking the boat somewhat with what I say, but, essentially, my aim is to put things right and improve the state of British tennis, if only for the sake of our juniors and their parents, who always start out with such high hopes.

If you care, as I do, I urge you to read my book, and react as you think fit.

FROM THE CO-AUTHOR

Whether you have little talent or loads of talent, Steve Kitcher will have you playing and looking like a proper tennis player in a very short space of time. As someone with a good club standard, he did more for me in a few lessons than other coaches have done in over forty years. I have never come across anybody who understands the mechanics of tennis like Steve. As a coach, he is the complete package, and should not be allowed just to ply his trade in the backwoods of Kent.

This book is essentially his book: my function, as a co-author with an academic background, has been to try and give it the style and polish it deserves.

Hopefully, something positive will result from our efforts.

A NOTE ABOUT THE TEXT

Throughout this book, for the purposes of style, 'he' embraces 'she', unless, of course, the feminine pronoun is clearly appropriate.

ACKNOWLEDGEMENTS

M̲y thanks must go to the many tennis enthusiasts who have encouraged me to complete this book.

Having learnt little on my first coaching qualification course - an LTA one - I am so grateful to the tutor of my second course, Piers Bastard, who cleverly adapted the USPTR coaching system, a worldwide method for teaching tennis, and gave me such wonderful tools with which to work. From this very comprehensive, and intensive, seventeen-day course, I was able to coach immediately with confidence, and in time develop my skills to give me an understanding of how to coach to my present standard. Without this course I may never have had a career in tennis, but, having completed more than twenty-five years of full-time coaching, I wish to thank so many people who have supported me along the way, and kept me going when many other coaches might have given up.

In particular I wish to name a few very special supporters who lost their lives at far too young an age. I am forever grateful to them and am a better person because of them. They are: Jim Mortimer, Tony Sanderson, Liz Addison, Roy Holgate and Fiona Walls. And from my own family: my niece Charlotte, who in 2014 lost her life in such appalling circumstances at the tender age of twenty-nine, and my mother Paulette, both of whom were very keen tennis players.

As a player, I never believed I was that good at tennis. I certainly did not master it in the way I did table tennis. But only starting to play tennis seriously in my mid-twenties, I know that, without the wonderful practice sessions I regularly had with Julian Godfrey, I would never have reached a good county standard, nor would I have understood the game so well or gained sufficient confidence to consider a career in coaching. I am therefore most grateful to Julian as well.

British Tennis:

Game, Set & ... MESS!

INTRODUCTION

This book is about the reality of British tennis.

We may have a Wimbledon Champion in Andy Murray, but we have precious little else at the top of the world game: a couple of women players who are worthy of the top 100 in singles, and a few reasonably successful doubles specialists in this much less demanding, and less important, format of the game, and that is it, and has been it for as long as my co-author and I can remember – and that is a long, long time.

Across the Channel, France not only has a Wimbledon Champion in Marion Bartoli, but also around a dozen men and women in the top 50, and even more in the top 100, and a good number of successful doubles players who also play singles at a world-class level.

On this side of the Channel, the Lawn Tennis Association (LTA), the governing body of the sport in the UK, have had untold millions at their disposal over the last forty years or so, with the British public in the wings absolutely aching for them to succeed, and they have still failed to produce world-class tennis players. Their record is even worse than that of many third-world countries.

Quite simply, there must be something wrong, and very seriously wrong. This book – self-financed – has been written with the aim of delving into the mess, explaining it, and providing the solution.

If you are interested in the sport of tennis in Great Britain, or sport in general for that matter, or just curious to know more, the pages contained within will give you an unexpected, but unerring, insight into the problem.

The Lawn Tennis Association do many things well, but there is definitely a huge mess when it comes to producing professional tennis players.

There is, inevitably, much criticism to be found between the covers of this book, but, in the end, as you will see, the criticism is essentially constructive.

As the author, my sincere hope is that some good will come out of my efforts.

CHAPTER 1

Firstly, something about me and where I am coming from

I have been a full-time tennis coach for over twenty-five years and have always been acutely aware of the failure of British tennis to produce top-class players. As stated in the Introduction, compared to many other countries, our record at getting players into the top 100 is appalling, and, it can be argued, has got even worse in recent years.

Gradually, over the period of time I have been coaching, I have come to realise what the problem is, and have been encouraged by the people I have met through my job, including coaches, to put my solution in writing. I am most grateful to them for their encouragement, and especially to Colin Thorne, a friend from the academic world, a tennis enthusiast himself and a former full-time coach, who has given this book the polish and style that it would otherwise have lacked.

As regards my own tennis and interest in the sport, I started playing with a friend at the age of eleven. I enjoyed it so much that I soon joined my local village club and found I was able to beat boys who were older, and I even had some success at singles and doubles in local tournaments. As I had no access to coaching, and little guidance from my parents, I remained at my small village club, and was also made captain of my school tennis team.

When I was nearly fifteen, however, I was spotted playing table tennis and my world was transformed: someone saw that I had some talent and strongly urged my father to let me play in the local league for adults. The upshot was that I played no tennis for the next six years – I just competed and lived for table tennis, winning many local tournaments; I also represented the county, as I was ranked in the top 3, and often found myself up against international players; in addition, I was invited to take part in several exhibition matches against the likes of Chester Barnes, the former English number 1.

My love for tennis, though, never really diminished, although my experiences with high-level table tennis were incredibly satisfying and enjoyable. Later on, as a tennis coach, I found that the time I had spent competing on the ping-pong table, coupled with the fact that I had also qualified as a table tennis coach, helped me considerably when giving advice about how to play competitively, especially with regard to the preparation needed for important matches, and also the psychology required.

I therefore went back to playing just tennis at the age of twenty-five, joining Alverstoke tennis club in Hampshire. I shall always be grateful for the wonderful practice sessions I had with Julian Godfrey, who was later to be the coach of the British number 2 and successful Wimbledon player, Chris Wilkinson. I learnt so much by copying Julian's stylish shots, and, two years down the line, he and I made the county team as the numbers 1 and 2.

It is interesting how we both, as adults, overtook all

the serious juniors around us who were receiving endless hours of coaching and playing in loads of tournaments, but never managed to join us in the county team. As you read through the book you will find out, in no uncertain terms, why they failed.

I played lots of county matches, managed to become county champion, as I had in table tennis, won the Ministry of Defence National Championships, and also won many singles titles in local tournaments and at club level. I achieved a national tennis rating of -4/6, which the Lawn Tennis Association later turned into 1.5 (as equivalent to -4/6), and subsequently changed to 3.1, again as an equivalent rating to the previous two that I had had. The further you get into the book, the more you will get used to the LTA's propensity for changing things.

At the age of thirty I decided to give up my boring job at the Ministry of Defence in order to become a tennis coach.

The first qualification I obtained was that of LTA Elementary Coach, which at the time was the first step on the ladder of the coaching system run by the governing body of British tennis, the aforementioned LTA (Lawn Tennis Association).

The thirty-six-hour course I did was a new one, and was supposed to be much more comprehensive and thorough than anything that had previously been on offer. However, I was so horrified at the poor quality of it all that I decided to search elsewhere for some better guidelines. Quite simply, I realised that I did not have a clue as to how to coach tennis! It was such a contrast to the much better training I had received when qualifying as a table tennis coach.

Fortunately, I found what I was looking for when I enrolled on a coaching course run by a Kenyan called Piers Bastard. Piers based his teaching on the Professional

Tennis Registry (PTR) course that originated in the USA, and which was still relatively new to this country.

It was far more precise and methodical than the LTA course I had been on, and, as a relatively young and very inexperienced tennis coach, I really felt I was finally learning how to teach properly. I was awarded the top qualification of 'Professional'. Only one other person in the UK has ever been deemed by Piers as being worthy of such heights.

By way of explanation, the PTR, founded in the USA in 1976 by the South African Denis Van der Meer, and backed by Billie Jean King, is a very successful coaching organisation. At the time of writing it has some 14,000 teachers worldwide, and members in 110 countries.

Subsequent to my success on the PTR course, I was asked to be an examiner for them on several occasions, and was also a PTR Regional Director for a while.

However, I still felt that I had a lot to learn, so I was constantly seeking to further my knowledge. To this end, I attended many more coaching courses on different aspects of tennis, run by both the PTR and the LTA; I also undertook a trip to the USA, where I picked the brains of all the top coaches I could find: people like the German Richard Schonborn, once voted the number 1 coach in Europe; Nick Bollettieri, number 1 in the world, according to many, and owner of the hugely successful tennis academy in Florida; Jim 'Coach' Verdieck, the most successful coach in American collegiate tennis; Dennis Van der Meer, (founder of the PTR); Dr Jim Loehr, who was at the time considered to be the top sports psychologist for tennis, and many others, not so well known, but still great sources of information and expertise. The sum total of all these endeavours was absolutely invaluable in my development as a coach.

In my own time, I also carried out a meticulous video analysis of all the strokes in tennis, as played by the professionals, and discovered that all high-level players have the same basic technique for each stroke, even though the style of one player can be so different to that of another, which can mislead the onlooker into thinking that their techniques vary greatly. I might add that quite a few coaches and commentators on tennis are also misled: I can state quite categorically that their techniques do not vary, and that all the top players have certain common elements in each of their strokes. Using this knowledge, I have been able to develop my own system and method for teaching tennis quickly, effectively and easily.

As regards my own coaching career, I started working in 1986 at an indoor tennis centre. Seven of the eight boys I coached went on to take seven of the eight places in the top under-14 Kent county squad by the end of the year. They won numerous county titles between them, with one going on to win the National Parks under-18 singles title, and another had success on the lower professional tour in Europe (now called Futures). After a year, I left the indoor centre to coach at various clubs, country clubs, sports centres, and schools.

In 2006, fed up with being poorly treated and pushed around by committees and managers over a long period of time – you will find out in due course what coaches have to put up with! – I decided to take advantage of an opportunity that came my way.

With the help of a fellow coach and friend, I obtained a lease from the local council so that I could set up and run a tennis academy on two of the six courts in a local park.

Within three years the council recognised the value of what I was doing and invited me to run the whole tennis site for the local community. I had floodlights erected over four of the six newly-surfaced courts, and installed quality garden furniture and parasols.

The two groundsmen, previously based on site, were redeployed, a proper tennis booking system was set up, and open invites to mix-ins were offered to the general public in attractive surroundings.

When I handed the non-membership tennis academy over to one of my coaches recently, there were 600 users on my database. In 2012, my considerable efforts in bringing tennis to the local community, and also persuading the council to resurface every tennis court in all three parks of the borough, were rewarded when I was selected to run with the Olympic torch – something I shall always treasure.

During my time as a coach I was shortlisted for the job of Kent County Development Officer, but I had to voice my concerns during my interview when I realised I would be expected to follow strict guidelines and lose the independence I had enjoyed. I therefore withdrew myself as a candidate for the post.

A few years later, in 2004, I was shortlisted and interviewed at LTA headquarters for the position of Executive for the Coaching Department. Needless to say, I was not appointed, otherwise it would not have been necessary to write this book. I still hope against hope to improve the state of British tennis, despite the decades of failure we have all endured.

It is not up to me to say whether I am a good, bad or indifferent coach – that is for others to judge. However, in the interests of relevance to what is in this book, and on the advice of my co-author, I have to cast aside my English modesty and report that I have been complimented about my coaching system on many occasions by adults, juniors, their parents, and by many coaches who have sought my expertise and guidance.

What those who come to learn tennis with me usually have in common is their experience of receiving coaching elsewhere. They are therefore in a position to compare the way I teach with the way other coaches teach, and what they like is my very different approach to coaching and how effective it is. They are all impressed at how I assess a player, see the real weakness or weaknesses, identify the cause, and put it right with immediate results.

It is no different to that of a car mechanic who is given a vehicle to repair: he will identify the exact problem, rectify it, and have the car quickly back on the road in good working order.

In tennis it is not difficult, or should not be difficult, to identify why someone has a problem executing a certain shot, and then correcting it technically. In addition to this, I have a system for building an entire tennis game in the right order – something that is often overlooked by other coaches. Most operate in such a random and vague way, often covering many aspects of tennis in one lesson, that, when people come to me, they are struck by my very precise approach, using a method and system they have not encountered elsewhere. They are delighted with the quick progress they make, and say it is so different from, and better than, the other coaching they have received.

At one coaches' conference, many years ago, I acquired the nickname of 'Mr. Technique'. The other coaches were teasing me, of course, but I took it as a compliment, and was, and am, quite happy with how they referred to me. In my opinion, there is no point being confident and quick on the tennis court, getting your tactics right, and having the stamina for a long three-set match on a hot day, if, when you get to the ball, you cannot play the shot required. Technique is simply everything. The other aspects of tennis only become important **after** you have perfected it.

Interestingly, Andy Murray has said that, during his time in Spain as a fifteen and sixteen year-old, all he did was work on his game – other things, like being supremely fit and actually working out, came much later.

I have come to realise that my philosophy for tennis coaching is the reason for the many positive and favourable reactions I have had over the years from those who have learnt with me.

Although it is true many believe that the mental side, or being in the right frame of mind, is all-important in pressure situations, I can assure you, as a qualified sports psychologist, who has not only helped tennis players with their mental approach, but also professional golfers, this is not so. The most crucial thing you need is a solid technique that you can rely on time and time again. You may be shaking with tension and nervousness, but the right technique will so often see you through.

It is very nice to be praised by one's customers. However, what is far more important to me, and of great relevance to the book regarding the mess we are in, is the fact that many juniors, who have started with me and gone on to achieve early success in tournaments, are taken away by the LTA system for subsidised training. They are then quite simply failed by the coaching programme. Their progress is limited, they get nowhere, and just give up. Indeed, I have heard the same damning complaint from other coaches around the country who have had similar experiences.

The following will serve as examples of what I am

saying.

Quite by chance, on the golf course where I had gone to play, I met two juniors, still in their teens, whom I had coached a few years previously. They had both achieved some early tournament success, and had moved on to LTA training.

However, they told me that they had given up tennis completely, so disillusioned were they with the coaching and the guidance they had received since leaving my much more precise tuition. They both felt they were not learning any more, and were not making progress, so they decided to take up golf and have some lessons. They immediately found the teaching much better and more satisfying, saying that it was very similar to what they had experienced with me, and the weaker golfer of the two had already reached a handicap of 4.

In another case, a mother pulled her promising son out of tennis because of the disorganisation she witnessed at LTA training, and also during his first tournaments. She thanked me for my reliable, efficient and very effective coaching, which she claimed had undoubtedly got her son to a high standard so quickly, but, after such bad experiences, she had decided that he should pursue his other love, which was music.

And here is just one of many examples: the father of a top junior, who left my coaching to attend under-12 LTA training, asked the LTA coach if his son could be promoted to the under-14 squad instead, so superior was he to the next best in his age group.

The youngster, Tim Wilcher, had already proved himself by being considered the number 1 at Bisham Abbey from the twenty top boys in the country who had come through the Cliff Richard 'Search for a Star' scheme, which had sifted him down from 10,000 entrants.

When the father's request for him to play with the older boys was turned down, he took his son away to concentrate on hockey, the father's main sport, commenting that the LTA sessions were a waste of time: the coaching was poor and wishy-washy, and his son was never stretched, since he had to play endless matches against the other under-12s, with hardly the loss of a single game.

The junior in question is still one of the greatest talents I have been fortunate enough to coach in all my years of teaching tennis, but I needed the LTA system to play its part and, in effect, take over the development of my pupil. Sadly, and perhaps tragically, this did not happen.

On LTA coaches' courses I have been instructed to feed promising youngsters into the bigger system, and, on principle, I have been quite willing to do so, but the above is a typical example of why it is a waste of time. Talented juniors are simply passed into a system of failure. In other sports, such juniors usually blossom as they move up the ladder.

Working as I did in the local park may have been fulfilling, but it was also frustrating that most talented juniors who are serious about tennis tend to head straight for the bigger clubs and indoor centres, where they believe they will get the best guidance.

Unfortunately, when these juniors eventually fail, they think it is their fault: they simply conclude that they were not good enough, or that they did not work hard enough, when the truth is they have actually been let down by the LTA system, because the right programmes are simply not in place.

Jamie, the more talented sibling of the Murray family, attended an LTA academy full-time in Cambridge at the age of twelve and, within eight months, his game had fallen apart; his brother, Andy, chose to attend an academy in

Spain. No more needs to be said!

As you may have gathered already, there is nothing fancy about me – I simply come from the grass roots of British tennis. This is the world I know and understand. I have seen and experienced what goes on at this lowest of levels, which, in the past, has often been overlooked, or just ignored, by the powers that be at the LTA.

However, since Sport England's £10.3m of funding for 'growing the sport' was withheld from the LTA for the 2013-2017 cycle, resulting in the organisation being 'put on notice', their attitude to grass-roots tennis has changed radically. There have been, and will be, massive national campaigns to get 'more people playing tennis, more often', as the current mantra has it. Free tennis sessions galore, all over the place – in parks, clubs, schools, universities, colleges of further education and, it seems, anywhere else you can think of.

There is, of course, nothing wrong in trying to increase the number of people playing tennis in the UK – it is what we all want and is very healthy for the sport. But quantity is not the equivalent of quality, and, as you read through the chapters of this book, I hope that you will come to a full awareness of my reasons for going into print in this way. Grass roots? Yes, but the roots must be sound and strong for something significant to grow out of them.

Unfortunately, the ideas and proposals in this book may well be ignored because I am not a famous name in British tennis, although I could try and lay some claim to fame by saying that I appeared a few years ago in a Sky Sports documentary, made by the former top 100 player, Mark Petchey, highlighting the problems in British tennis.

On another occasion, in 2001, I was interviewed by a

sports journalist who asked me who was going to be the star of the future, and I said, 'Roger Federer,' as he played more to my coaching system than any other player at the time. It was fully two years before Roger hit the headlines and started to create what was eventually to become *Planet Federer*. I still have the article containing my quote, with the date on, of course, in case anyone does not believe me.

And finally, as a claim to fame, in the English Open table tennis championships, I once found myself playing against the Japanese player, Hasegawa – the former world singles champion.

I do, however, think that the above attempt at trying to convince people I am a little bit famous, and therefore should be listened to, is misguided, because it should not be a criterion for judging this book. In fact, I am able to see the problems of British tennis from a very different vantage point to most people who are generally asked their opinion on the subject. Often they are former world-class players, whom, of course, I fully respect and admire, but the truth is, they live in a completely different world from me. None of them has had the experiences that I have gone through at the very bottom of British tennis for over twenty-five years, nor have they seen the mess that exists there.

Using the analogy of a mechanic again, I could well be likened to such a person building a sports car from scratch – I know perfectly how it all works. Tim Henman, Greg Rusedski, and suchlike, are the equivalent of the top racing drivers: they simply do not know what is going on underneath them – they just drive the car with great skill and flair. But underneath, unfortunately, is where the problems lie in British tennis.

However, should my book be dismissed by those with the power to act, what I have written will at least serve as a point of reference, if or when, and I suspect, and expect, the latter, we are in the same situation in three, five, or ten years' time.

Please read on – it is not all doom and gloom, but there is most certainly a mess to be sorted out.

CHAPTER 2

The significance of 2013

For the purposes of this book, 2013 was not significant because Andy Murray won Wimbledon, but because Roger Draper, the Chief Executive and man at the very top of the Lawn Tennis Association, announced he was leaving his post at the end of September that year. This was despite saying in an interview given to GlobalSportsJobs on 15th November, 2012: 'I want to continue to lead the transformation of British tennis to ensure that all the objectives we set out in the 2006 ten-year Blueprint for British tennis are achieved.'

When the announcement came in March, 2013, the four Sky Sports tennis commentators, Mark Petchey, Barry Cowan, Andrew Castle and Peter Fleming, all ex-professional players and all familiar with the sport in Great Britain, were unanimous in saying that British tennis was in a very bad way. This was, of course, before Andy Murray had won Wimbledon, but, strictly speaking, that does not change things at all.

Also in 2013, Phil Smith, the Director of Sport England, the public body that decides how to distribute money to different sports on behalf of the taxpayer and the lottery, threatened to withdraw funding to the tune of £17.4m, having already reduced it in December, 2012, from £24.5m, if the LTA did not increase significantly the numbers playing tennis by December, 2013, which we now know they failed to do. Phil Smith also said that, if the LTA could not do the job, Sport England would find someone else who could.

As a result of this stinging criticism, as mentioned in the last chapter, the LTA upped their efforts even more in 2013 and desperately tried to persuade all and sundry to play tennis – in schools, parks, community centres, or anywhere, for that matter. However, the unbelievable thing is that the attempts to increase participation in the sport had started several years previously, also with a great sense of urgency, and, by 2013, they had still not produced satisfactory results. One does wonder about 2014, with multiple initiatives afoot to boost numbers yet again, including the painting of park courts in bright colours to make them more eye-catching.

As if the highly critical stance of Sport England were not enough, in December 2012, the labour peer, Baroness Billingham of Banbury, Chair of the All-Party Tennis Group, referring to the low numbers playing tennis, concluded: 'The LTA is one of the wealthiest sporting organisations in the country, and it's my honest and genuine opinion that they are useless'. She also referred to Roger Draper's salary of £640,000 a year as 'unthinkable'.

And yet there was so much hope around in 2009, when the life assurance and pensions company, Aegon UK, became the Lead Partner of British tennis and undertook to invest massively in the game. Aegon's Marketing Director at the time, Steve Clode, optimistically described tennis in this country as a 'fast-growing' sport.

2013 was certainly a significant year, especially with the

departure of a Chief Executive who was expecting to be in the post until at least 2016. But we are still in a mess.

My sincere hope is that the new Chief Executive of the LTA, the Canadian Michael Downey, will be sufficiently down-to-earth to make the time to read this book, containing the thoughts and ideas of a humble and lowly grass-roots coach, with more than twenty-five years' experience of life at the bottom of British tennis. He will then realise that a complete rethink and an entirely different approach are so desperately needed in one particular and very important area of the sport.

Of course, I very much hope that other people will read this book as well, and perhaps see that it has some merit. And some might even actively support me.

CHAPTER 3

The ingredients necessary for success

As I wrote at the end of Chapter 1, it is not all doom and gloom, and one of the reasons is that British tennis already possesses a number of ingredients necessary for success.

Firstly, the LTA are the envy of the sporting world with a yearly income of over £60m. They are particularly lucky because around half of this figure is guaranteed every year by the Wimbledon Championships (£37.8m in 2012). The rest comes from other sources of funding, such as Sport England and sponsorships of different kinds. Compared to the governing bodies of tennis of most other countries, the LTA are fabulously wealthy. The Polish tennis federation, for example, had to make do with just £990,000 in 2012.

When Roger Draper was appointed as the Chief Executive in 2006, he started to make radical changes to the structure of the LTA in an attempt to turn it into a modern-day business organisation. In 2009 he managed to add yet more money to the coffers by brokering a multi-year sponsorship deal, in effect, until 2017, with the life assurance and pensions company, Aegon UK, as mentioned in the previous chapter. As a result, Aegon

UK now sponsor British tennis from top to bottom: from the pre-Wimbledon grass-court tournaments of Queen's, Eastbourne and Birmingham, tournaments at junior and club level, the funding of promising players, right through to the grass-roots and parks programmes. They have also sponsored tennis on Sky Sports.

It is quite an achievement to have all this money available during the worst economic crisis in living memory. What this means, in effect, is that any British player who shows great promise has funding guaranteed to help pay for training, travelling to tournaments, often with a coach, both here and abroad, and has money for accommodation expenses as well, etc. Even at the age of eight a player with outstanding talent can be awarded funding.

What a contrast to the situation of certain players who were not lucky enough to be born in Great Britain. The Pole, Jerzy Janowicz, semifinalist at Wimbledon in 2013, could not travel to the Australian Open in January 2012, because he did not have enough money; the Russian top 100 player, Evgeny Donskoy, is only playing on the professional circuit because he had, and still has, the financial backing of a Russian billionaire on the recommendation of former top player Marat Safin; and sleeping rough to save money, as the Croat, Ivan Dodig, used to do sometimes on the Futures and Challenger tours, just would not be allowed to happen to any of our players.

It is also worth pointing out that, since 2006, funding in Great Britain has been much better organised by the LTA, with everything made very transparent on a special website. In addition, a young player can use his funding to help pay for the coach of his choice, and, for those hoping to be given some financial help, targets to aim for are also clearly shown on the website.

Apart from all the money at the disposal of the LTA, the training facilities we have must be mentioned as an obvious ingredient necessary for success. The National Tennis Centre at Roehampton, opened in 2007 by the Queen, and now the headquarters of the LTA, has everything that a top tournament player requires: four types of court on which to practise (22 courts in total), world-class gymnasium and sports science centre, performance analysis, psychology and physiotherapy services, medical support, nutrition advice, and so on, and so on. They have even installed Hawk-Eye on one of the courts! At a cost of £40m one would not expect anything less.

And for those juniors who have some talent, and are serious about training to be top tennis players, there are 93 Performance Centres around the country, with teams of coaches running the daily programmes. They are made up of four International Performance Centres, seventeen High Performance Centres, and seventy-two Performance Centres, the latter being the starting point for the youngest juniors, and usually based at good clubs and indoor centres. The whole system is backed up by a very good Talent Identification Programme.

A third ingredient for success is the amazingly supportive attitude to British tennis of the general public in the UK. When Roger Draper said in 2006 that he wanted to make tennis the second most popular sport in Great Britain after football, it would be easy to dismiss this ambitious statement as just another impossible goal, of which there have been many coming from the LTA over the years.

An excellent illustration of this support comes from 1997, when Greg Rusedski, a player of Canadian origin(!), was voted the BBC Sports Personality of the Year on the back of reaching the US Open final in the September. With the majority of tennis votes going to Greg, there were still enough tennis fans to vote Tim Henman second in the BBC poll. The Canadian had lost the US Open final, which incidentally was of poor quality, and Tim Henman had never reached a Grand Slam final. Neither player was ever ranked higher than fourth in the world, the pair never teamed up to win anything in doubles, nor did they threaten to win the Davis Cup, where each team only requires two players in order to do well, and yet, in competition with the high achievers of other sports that year, they still came first and second. All in all, a staggering endorsement of British tennis from the great British public, and only one of them was English.

And, of course, in December, 2013, Andy Murray won the accolade hands-down, getting more votes than the other nine contenders put together, having attracted in July the biggest TV audience ever for the BBC that year for his Wimbledon triumph. The BBC could have made things much easier for themselves by simply flying over to Miami to give him the award without even bothering with all the rigmarole of a vote. And probably no one would have complained.

It has to be said that the support, and indeed love, for tennis in Great Britain is quite remarkable. Tournaments like Queen's are virtually sold out on the first day, whilst abroad, at a similar tournament, the stands would be practically empty; at Wimbledon, 10,000 people queue overnight in the hope of getting a ticket, families organise their holidays around the event just to be able to see it on TV, and in many cases they do not even play tennis; at the eight-day singles and doubles ATP World Tour Finals in November at the O2 arena in London, the biggest indoor tournament in the world, each one of the fourteen sessions before the final is practically full, meaning that almost 34,000 people attend every day, and, by the end of the tournament, the organisers are not far short of the 250,000 capacity for the event. It is not surprising that the original five-year deal for London has been extended to 2015. In short, the appetite for tennis in the UK seems quite insatiable.

Roger Draper was not perhaps being over-ambitious after all in wanting to make tennis the second most popular sport in Great Britain. Unfortunately, it did not come to pass, but the ingredients are undoubtedly there.

Add to all this the obsession of the media with covering anything British that moves on a tennis court showing promise and talent, not to mention the blanket coverage of the Wimbledon fortnight on TV and radio, and the popular Sky Sports and Eurosport presentations of tournaments throughout the year, and we have a picture that is so full of goodwill and desire for success that one has to wonder why the landscape is so barren in British terms.

Quite frankly, we should not be in a mess, but we are. Hardly anyone in the top 100, male or female, to make full use of the £40m National Tennis Centre at Roehampton, ninety-five Performance Centres that seem incapable of producing anyone of real quality, and a grass-roots programme that appears so impressive, with all the money and energy going into it, but is simply not delivering in terms of quality.

Unfortunately, in my opinion, most of what is happening to improve things is flawed. It is no coincidence that what is wrong at the bottom of British tennis, and above it for that matter, is reflected in the lack of success right at the top. I refer you to later chapters for much more comment on these matters.

But, first, please read the next chapter because it provides a fascinating insight into the situation here, as seen and studied by an American sports journalist.

CHAPTER 4

There is no reason for British tennis to fail

The title of this chapter was the conclusion that an American sports journalist came to after carrying out a comprehensive and thorough examination of British tennis and its inability to produce top players. The article, long and very detailed, appeared some fifteen years ago in a tennis magazine which I came across quite by chance one day. Unfortunately, I could not keep the magazine, so I cannot name the journalist or the publication, but I would be more than happy to rectify this should the relevant details ever come to light.

At the time I thought I knew what was wrong with British tennis, but I was not absolutely sure. This article turned any doubts I had into certainties and, it could be said, eventually prompted me to write this book.

In the article the writer examined every facet of the British way of life in order to try and understand why, if you are British and want to succeed in the world of professional tennis, you are almost certainly doomed to failure. I remember the words so well.

He suggested that there must be something about Great Britain which will always stop you reaching the top, however hard you try. But every time he found a possible reason, whether it was our culture, size of population, numbers playing, tennis as taught or not taught in schools, diet, facilities available, lack of indoor courts, not enough money, climate, coaching system, number of coaches, too few competitions, lack of talent/opportunities, television coverage, and so on, he could always find one country, if not a number of countries, worse off than Great Britain in that particular department. And those countries that were more disadvantaged than the UK were still far more successful at producing world-class tennis players.

He even considered that perhaps Britain suffered in tennis terms by being an island, cut off from mainland Europe, but then he found other islands that were more successful at tennis than we were, so that possible reason was ruled out too.

He had to conclude, as the title of this chapter suggests, that there is no reason for British tennis to fail.

In one sense, this is very good news, but the inescapable truth is that we have never had a production line of world-class players, so it must be down to something else that the American journalist was not aware of – hence, this book.

My rejection of the reasons given over the decades for the failures in British tennis stems in part from my chance encounter with the findings of the said journalist, but only in part, because I was already working my way to the same conclusion from my own experiences – no reason to fail, except for…

After reading the article with great fascination and much care, I realised the writer had missed something, even though he had carried out an impressively wide-ranging survey. He had, in fact, considered this particular aspect of British tennis, but had glossed over it somewhat - unintentionally I am sure - and thought that it was in good working order because what was on offer seemed perfectly sound and appropriate. Had he delved more deeply and seen something of what I have seen over the years, he would have indeed found the reason for the constant failings of British tennis.

The aspect in question is what I referred to in Chapter 1: i.e. what happens at grass-roots level and the development of players thereafter. The American had drawn a blank in his quest for a reason but, in so doing, had enabled me to see clearly what I had suspected for some time – it was, in effect, my light bulb moment.

What he had missed is absolutely crucial, in my opinion, to the process of producing top performers in any sport. We are very good at it when it comes to golf, cycling, cricket, snooker..., but quite useless at it when it comes to tennis. In later chapters I set out fully my thoughts on this absolutely fundamental point. The LTA have also missed it, otherwise they would have put it right. It goes without saying, of course, that they did not miss it on purpose, but the truth is – they are simply not aware of the mess that exists.

I am convinced that Tim Henman, who spent his formative years in tennis in Great Britain, and not in another country like Andy Murray, would have won Wimbledon if this one aspect had been in place when he was an aspiring junior and trying to learn his trade.

What happened was the following: he asked for help to improve his serve, but it was not forthcoming. Tim Henman himself has openly criticised British coaching on this point, because all he needed to reach the pinnacle was a more powerful delivery, and, to put it bluntly, the LTA failed him when he was still only a nineteen year-old.

It is a tribute to his incredible talent and tennis brain that he managed to reach four Wimbledon semi-finals, and two other Grand Slam semi-finals (the US and the French), and also held his place in the top 10 in the world, almost without interruption and without a really big serve, for seven years. Unfortunately, the other juniors of his generation were let down, like so many, by the LTA set-up, and fell by the wayside.

The American journalist thought that everything was fine; those at the top of British tennis think that everything is fine. But, below the surface, everything is far from fine – in fact, it is in desperate need of a complete overhaul if we are to get out of the mess we are in.

A judgement most harsh, you may think, and I must emphasise here that what I am referring to is but a small part of all the things that the LTA do, and do very well, I might add.

It is just that this one aspect is in a real mess, and it is an aspect that is absolutely crucial when it comes to producing world-class players. Up to now, no one has seen the need to try and sort it out. Or perhaps nobody knows how to put it right? In essence, this book has been written to this end.

First, however, I would like to describe some of the LTA's efforts over the years to find the answers to the problems of British tennis. Although they have all failed, it is important to consider them for a better understanding of the whole situation.

All this you will find in the next chapter.

CHAPTER 5

Background to the mess

For well over forty years the LTA have tried so hard to get it right. I sometimes wish we were German – such a mess would have been sorted out almost before it had started. And what about if the enormous yearly profits from the Wimbledon Championships had suddenly been withdrawn? That would have concentrated a few minds!

My co-author remembers a headline on the front page of a tennis publication in the heyday of Jimmy Connors, who is now over sixty years of age: *Why can't Great Britain produce better players?* There was no definitive answer then, and there has been no definitive answer since. It was even a mystery that eluded the diligent research of the American journalist, as described in the last chapter.

The LTA were, and are still, so desperate for success that there was even talk at one time of trying to persuade a young Novak Djokovic to adopt British nationality, although I am not sure whether this was media-driven, or whether it did, in fact, emanate from the LTA. The truth is always so hard to come by.

What manna from heaven it must have been for them when a young Greg Rusedski came over from Canada to join a slightly younger Tim Henman and provide a world-class twosome for British tennis and our Davis Cup team. That kept the media quiet for a while, and also gave the impression that we were not so bad after all.

During Wimbledon rain breaks we have all heard top ex-professional tennis players from overseas being asked about the lamentable state of British tennis and why this is so. Of course, they can only guess at the reasons because they are not at all familiar with tennis in Britain – what goes on at grass-roots level, how a typical British tennis club operates, etc. – but, out of politeness and a desire to show they have an opinion, they will refer to 'the poor climate', 'a lack of mental strength' in our leading players, a need 'to get more people playing', etc. It was so refreshing once to hear one such player being completely honest by saying that he had absolutely no idea, since he did not live here.

And the British ex-professionals – also with limited knowledge of grass-roots tennis and how a typical LTA club operates – do not throw much light on the matter either: they jump on each other's bandwagon and, anyway, tend to change their tack from one year to the next, according to what the latest excuse is that is going the rounds.

'We have been having this conversation for too long.' someone said during the 2013 Wimbledon. Indeed we have, and it is high time we did something about it. Thank goodness for the roof over Centre Court – at least it ensures that there is considerably less time now for such banal chat.

For decades, then, no one has been able to arrive at a definitive answer, otherwise the problem would have been solved by now. This book, though, does have the definitive answer, but, whether it is acted upon or not, is, of course, another matter entirely.

As stated at the beginning of the chapter, the LTA have tried so hard, so desperately hard, to find a solution that you could almost feel sorry for them if it were not for all the millions upon millions of pounds that they have spent, and in effect wasted, on schemes and programmes that have brought no tangible results.

The LTA certainly care, there is absolutely no doubt about that, but, over the years, they have gone, even lurched, from one so-called solution to another. Once an idea has run its course, it is simply binned and something else is tried. It has been akin to observing politicians trying to sort out the NHS or Education: one reform after another, one change of direction after another, all costing millions, and all pointing to the highly unpleasant truth that they do not really know what to do, but they must be seen to be doing something, otherwise too many questions will be asked, and heads might even have to roll.

In the 1980s and 90s the LTA kept saying that the solution to all our problems would be to produce one truly world-class player, preferably a Grand Slam champion like Bjorn Borg or Boris Becker. A Briton, with a real chance of winning Wimbledon, for all of us to see on our TV screens, they said, would automatically lead to a boom in British tennis – we would simply be inundated with top players. And quite a few tennis enthusiasts went along with this, but I did not, because I was gradually becoming aware, from around the early 90s, of the real problem in British tennis – the grass roots, as you have probably gathered by now.

In any case, there was more than a hint that this was not the solution, since Sue Barker won the French Open in 1976, and Virginia Wade won Wimbledon in 1977, the Queen's Jubilee Year, no less, and there was no subsequent explosion of talented youngsters coming on to the scene.

And, of course, in the 90s and the early years of the

present century, we had Tim Henman, who, with his exciting serve-volley game and enormous talent, reached four semi-finals at the All England Club, was statistically the most successful Wimbledon player of all time not to have won a Grand Slam title, created *Henmania* in the process and a hill that is still named after him, and once again no revival in British tennis was forthcoming.

Now we have Andy Murray, probably the greatest British tennis player of all time, finally winning Wimbledon for us all, and yet, incredibly, the result of this magnificent achievement has seen the numbers playing tennis in the UK actually going down!

As I said in the Introduction, we may have a Wimbledon champion, but the reality is that this will not make the slightest difference because we do not have the right programmes in place. Undoubtedly, more youngsters will now try to get involved in the sport, but, sadly and inevitably, they will be disappointed and so will British tennis.

In fact as long ago as 1996, I was told by an ever-optimistic LTA: 'We think we now have the right programmes in place.'

Quite frankly, for far too long it has all been a question of five-year programmes replacing other five-year programmes with monotonous regularity, or one idea being quickly replaced by another as soon as it is realised that the current plan is not delivering and has little chance of doing so.

We are still waiting, of course, for miracles to happen, just as we are still waiting for British tennis to be transformed by the construction, which has now taken place, of loads of indoor courts – yet another solution that did not deliver.

Despite this constant and almost criminal lack of success,

the impression they have preferred to give over the years is one of, 'We at the LTA know best'. But in July of 2000 they let their guard down and gave us a glimpse of how desperate they really were. The British Davis Cup Team had just lost to Ecuador on the grass at Wimbledon. The deciding rubber had been won by a seventeen year-old Ecuadorean, with just three weeks' experience of playing on grass, and who subsequently never achieved anything in world tennis.

John Crowther, the Chief Executive of the LTA at the time, asked the public on Number One court at Wimbledon, where the tie had been played and with the TV cameras still rolling, to write to him with any ideas they had for improving the awful state of British tennis.

Thousands wrote in, including me, and, to my surprise, I was invited to the LTA board room at the Queen's Club in London to take part in the discussion on what could be done to get out of the mess. I have to admit at this juncture that I was truly shocked at what transpired in the meeting because I realised, fully for the first time, just how out of touch the top people at the LTA were with what was really going on in British tennis.

Around the table, apart from those representing the LTA, and this included Roger Draper, who soon after left to become Head of Sport England, and, a few years later, to replace Mr Crowther as the next Chief Executive, were some very well-known and influential people – among others, Trevor Brooking from the football world and representing Sport England, the Head of BBC Sport and the Head of Sky Sports.

I happened to sit next to a very influential person in Patrice Hagueleur, a Frenchman who had been appointed to help sort out our problems, having had considerable success in tennis in his home country.

45

I was allowed two minutes to say what I thought, i.e. the problems were at grass-roots level and, as soon as I finished, the man sitting next to me – the aforesaid Frenchman – took me to task and said he completely disagreed. He added that he had seen some coaching at clubs around the country and thought everything was in order. All the others in the room seemed reluctant to speak against the views of Monsieur Hagueleur and disagreed with my ideas as well, except for one person – Sue Mappin, the former National Women's Team Manager, with a special interest in community tennis in parks and schools. Her knowledge of, and familiarity with, the grass roots must have come into play when she interjected on my behalf: 'I'm sorry, but I think Steve is making a very valid point.' I was, of course, very grateful for some support at least.

As I have already said, I was truly shocked at the ignorance shown by the LTA about the problems at grass-roots level – problems that I knew only too well existed because I had been there for many years. They assumed that everything was fine, just like the American journalist in the previous chapter 'There is no reason for British tennis to fail', and again like the Frenchman, Patrice Hagueleur, who had observed some of the coaching at club level, as already stated.

What was happening around the country was being implemented, of course, by trained coaches, and all seemed well, but, as you will presently see, in reality it was, and is, far from well. In addition, coming from France, Patrice Hagueleur would have assumed that the grass-roots programmes here were similar, or, at least, looked similar, to those in his own country, and did not need any attention, although I still cannot quite work out why people born here, occupying key positions at the LTA, were unaware of what was going on, except possibly Sue Mappin.

I had a one-to-one chat with Patrice Hagueleur after the meeting, and it was quite clear to me that he was not at all on the same wavelength as I was with regard to the grass roots in this country. He simply did not understand.

The Frenchman, on a very high salary of course, promised to do great things for British tennis. He said he would achieve the 3 fives: within five years he would get five British men and five British women into the top 100.

He failed quite spectacularly. In fact, he resigned from his post on the 19th December, 2002, exactly twelve days before his five-year deadline expired. Before he slipped back to France for Christmas that year, never to return to work again in British tennis, the LTA paid great tribute to him, thanking him for all his efforts. No doubt, he may have improved things in some ways, but his highly ambitious promises, which were the sole reason for his appointment, had come to nothing – he had not even been close!

At the end of the crisis meeting at the Queen's Club in July, 2000, the Chief Executive, John Crowther, having heard everybody's contributions, concluded in very banal fashion that we should all seek to improve the state of British tennis by getting more juniors playing, improving facilities, and increasing the number of competitions. I use the word 'banal' because the conclusions arrived at were no more than a repetition of what had been tried in the past with no success.

'Get more juniors playing': this is the numbers game. If the right coaching and development programmes are not in place, it will not matter one iota if 10,000, 100,000, or 1,000,000 youngsters are playing tennis in Great Britain, because they will not have the tools to succeed at the higher levels of the sport. Cricket, for example, has considerably fewer adult players than tennis, 171,900 in 2009-2010, compared to 437,500 in tennis (from the Sport England Active People Survey), but we manage to produce a world-class England team in all formats of the game, despite some blips, and we have great depth as well. The simple reason for this is that young cricketers are coached far better right from the start – i.e. the grass roots and above.

'We must improve facilities,' the Chief Executive, John Crowther, said at the crisis meeting: again, it will not matter if we have more courts built in local parks, floodlights installed, or even more indoor centres of which there are already many, if the essential guidance is missing when youngsters are just starting out.

'Increase the number of competitions': this may give our juniors more match play experience, but does not change their fundamental weaknesses. This latter and most serious problem is dealt with fully later on in the book.

It seems that the LTA go back to the same old ideas time and time again when the pressure is on to do something: they simply revisit old solutions, or tweak them a little, put more money in, reorganise a bit here and there, and expect it all to work.

Unfortunately, it never works. After the Davis Cup débâcle against Ecuador in 2000, the same thing happened in 2010 – this time, against Lithuania, a country with a population of 3.2 million, and with a Tennis Federation having to make do at the time with a budget of just £90,000 a year. Sadly, nothing much had changed in British tennis, and a whole decade had gone by.

Sadly also, the LTA did not learn the lesson of their experiences with the Frenchman, Patrice Hagueleur, who promised so much and delivered so little. Soon after the arrival of Roger Draper as Chief Executive in 2006 they started bringing in many top foreign coaches, again on top salaries, of course, to lead us to the promised land.

This was in accordance with the Blueprint which Roger Draper and his headhunted team had put together soon after their arrival. The relevant section said: '...we have a track record of producing high-performing juniors who then fail to make the transition into winners in the senior game'. So all we needed was a 'world-class team of tennis professionals' to put it right. Very much a top-down approach was adopted here, but, then, there is nothing wrong with that if the base, at grass-roots level, is very sound.

Unfortunately, when Carl Maes, the former Belgian Federation Cup Captain and coach to Kim Clijsters in her formative years, arrived to take up his post as Head of Women's Tennis here, he soon recognised that, apart from the remarkable and unique Laura Robson, our under-14s were significantly below the standard required at international level.

I vividly recall Mr. Maes commenting along the lines that Britain's international juniors were only able to play as well as he would expect county juniors to play, and that our county juniors were basically still only playing at club-level standard. He further stated that the juniors were not developing correctly, a comment that I found particularly interesting, but not surprising, since I had experienced exactly the same thing when asked to coach a strong under-14 county squad for a while: they may have been talented, but I felt like taking them through my beginners' course in order to teach them the sound fundamentals they needed to have any chance of eventual success on the world stage.

The Belgian coach's assessment of Britain's best juniors was another example of how the LTA had misread the situation entirely and, once again, reality had eluded them, as in the crisis meeting referred to at the Queen's Club in 2000.

To put it simply, and starkly, our under-14s were not up to scratch because they had not been developed properly from the start.

There was, however, one exception, a piece of good news, at least, and this was Heather Watson, the winner of the British under-14s in 2006, and, three years later, the US Open Junior Champion. That, I am afraid, is the end of the good news, because she had not trained and learnt her tennis here, but, instead, had enrolled full-time at the Nick Bollettieri Academy in Florida at the age of twelve, and carried on there throughout her formative years. Very much like Andy Murray and his mother, therefore, Heather and her parents had decided to go for coaching outside this country in the quest for success at the top level.

Apart from Carl Maes, other big names came as well: the American, Brad Gilbert (erstwhile coach to Andre Agassi and Andy Roddick, and an ex-top 10 player himself); Paul Annacone (ex-top 10 and coach to Pete Sampras and Tim Henman); another Belgian, Steve Martins; the Swede, Peter Lundgren, and possibly one or two more whose names escape me. As far as I can tell, no perceptible improvement came about in British tennis as a result of this impressive influx, although Brad Gilbert did help a young Andy Murray to develop on a contract of £750,000 for forty weeks a year when the going rate for such a coach was £100,000, or less.

When the Scot decided to part with Brad Gilbert, there was still a year left on the American's contract, so the LTA gave him the job of travelling around the Futures and Challenger Circuit with Alex Bogdanovic, the British number 2 and ranked 161 at the time, in order to try and get him to 'pop'. This is American for make a breakthrough, in case you do not know. Unfortunately, Alex Bogdanovic did not pop, but the sight of the famous Brad Gilbert at these lower level tournaments did, at least, cause considerable merriment and comment among the other competitors, who were more used to seeing one man and his dog, if they were lucky, during their matches.

When Brad Gilbert left the LTA in September, 2008, he said he was sad to go – 'they are such nice people,' he added. Unfortunately, the 'nice people' at the LTA had got it wrong again. Their top-down approach was so ill-conceived that not one of the famous imports remains.

And how could such a policy succeed when the raw material these top international coaches had to work with was so lacking in quality?

Where there was quality, however, they did make a difference: Carl Maes helped Anne Keothavong to rise from her position outside the top 100 in 2008 to one of 48 in the rankings a year later (February, 2009), and Brad Gilbert gave a boost to Andy Murray, making him realise, among other things, that he had to get fitter and stronger in order to challenge the top players – advice that the Scot certainly took to heart. He is now as fit and strong as, if not fitter and stronger than, anyone in the top 10. He also learnt to use 'those damn drop shots' (B. Gilbert's words) more sparingly and much more effectively, and to stand back more when receiving 130-140mph serves.

Was it really necessary, though, to take on a foreign import, on £750,000, just to assist Andy Murray in this way? And to put Paul Annacone, for example, in charge of Men's Tennis in Britain when, as an American, he knew virtually nothing about how things worked here, was a decision so far removed from reality that I still cannot work out why it was made, unless the LTA thought that we had a number of potential Tim Henmans in the making – which we certainly did not.

Subsequently, Mr. Annacone moved on to coaching and advising Roger Federer – a position that fitted his world-class talents perfectly.

At least now we have a much more suitable incumbent in Leon Smith, a Scottish coach who comes from the lower end of tennis, and seems to be far more in touch with reality.

The 2006 Blueprint, which is basically a ten-year Action Plan that Roger Draper intended to see through to its conclusion, gives a good insight into how the new team at the LTA were proposing to solve the problems of British tennis. Reading through it, one cannot help but sense the great idealism, enthusiasm and tremendous energy of those who wrote it. Unfortunately, on so many fronts, they came up with ideas that have to be described as flawed because reality eluded them time and time again.

The Blueprint stated: '...players and parents blame the LTA', and made reference to 'coaches who lack credibility'. A massive and expensive Road Show was therefore organised to inspire coaches around the country and to give them extra training. Wherever the Road Show went, indoor tennis centres were hired for the day and lectures, on-court demonstrations with top British ex-professionals, and great food were all laid on.

In the lecture we were told, as we always are, regarding the training of juniors, that the number one priority for all our lessons had to be fun, and the word FUN was written on a board for us all to see. This is precisely why I have used the word 'flawed' above: coaches are basically teachers, and to tell them that the number one priority has to be FUN is a travesty of what they should be about.

If a schoolteacher presented such a priority to an Ofsted inspector, he would run the risk of instant dismissal, or, at the very least, would be required to undergo thorough retraining.

The number one priority for a serious tennis coach is to teach his pupil or class the different strokes of the sport, or whatever else is needed at the time, to enable progress to be made. Fun might well be part of the lesson at some stage – a good teacher will always be able to make such a judgement at the appropriate time – but, essentially, the coach's job is to teach, just like the schoolteacher in his classroom.

When I objected to the concept of fun being of such overriding importance, there was consternation from the speaker, along with gasps of disbelief from the twenty or so coaches in attendance, all of whom seemed to be in complete agreement with the idea of fun, fun, fun at all costs! At least, before dismissing my objection, the speaker asked me what I might consider to be of greater importance, to which I immediately replied: 'Progress.'

I was, though, totally outnumbered, and the speaker persisted in trying to convince me that coaching could only be considered 'good' if it was fun, and this key word remained at the top of the white board, in all its glory, for everyone to see and make a note of.

The consequences of this philosophy, if it can be called a philosophy, I have observed on many occasions. For example, I once saw an LTA-trained coach taking a class of youngsters and doing a very impressive job – on the surface, at least. The organisation and pace of the lesson were excellent, the children were kept occupied and moving, constantly running round, and having fun, of course. It is true that no one was bored, and parents and onlookers were most impressed. However, the one thing missing from it all was proper coaching: there was not one word of technical advice about how to hit the ball properly.

And I can assure you that all the children desperately needed advice on how to swing their racquets properly for any of the strokes they had to make, since they were constantly failing to control the ball. So the session – in no way could it be called coaching – was, in effect, a waste of time. The children were never going to develop sound basics, and were in danger of acquiring bad habits which, at a later date, could well be too ingrained for anyone to sort out. This is assuming, of course, that the juniors actually continued to attend coaching for much longer, with such little progress being made: why go on with something when you are not really learning much? The concept of FUN does have its limitations.

At grass-roots level I have had similar coaches wanting to work for me over the years when I have had a vacancy, but I have had to turn them down because they cannot coach properly – all they can do is keep everybody active and entertained. In the last chapter I suggested a complete overhaul was required: the lesson I have just described is a good illustration of why this is exactly what is needed.

How can British tennis make headway when there are coaches who have been so badly trained that they can provide fun, but not the know-how required for a sound tennis stroke?

If you ask a golf coach, i.e. a golf pro, what technical elements he looks for in a good golf swing, he will always be able to tell you; if you ask a tennis coach to describe what exactly is important in developing a sound technique for the forehand topspin, for example, he will invariably not be able to tell you. He will, it is true, sometimes have a guess at the answer, but, more often than not, he will come up with something too vague to be of real use, or will even say: 'It depends'. In other words, he is not at all sure because he has not been trained properly.

The reasons for this mess can perhaps be found in the complicated LTA coaching structure and the lack of a really solid core in the courses that are taught.

First, the coaching structure: it has been reorganised so many times in the last three decades that trying to follow and understand it is enough to give you a migraine.

Pre-1980, it was simple: Part 1 – for teaching beginners, Part 2 – for teaching more advanced players (spin on the ball, etc.), and Part 3 – for becoming a full-time professional coach and all that this entailed.

Of course, changes to coaching methods and training have inevitably to be made as a sport develops over time, but these changes can be, or could have been, incorporated within the simple to understand Part 1, 2 and 3 structure, even with the advent of mini tennis.

All the constant updating that has occurred in the last thirty years has resulted in nothing more than confusion. It does, though, give the casual observer the impression that the LTA are tireless in their efforts to incorporate the latest trends in their courses and maintain a real cutting edge.

The other two world-wide coaching systems available in the UK, the PTR (of US origin) and the RPT (of Spanish origin), both had, in the past, a much simpler structure, with – most importantly – a method for teaching the technique for the basic strokes, which was a vast improvement on what was, and is, taught on LTA courses.

While I used to be critical of both the PTR and the RPT for the shortness of their qualification courses and the weakness of their examination processes, things have changed in recent years, but not necessarily for the better.

In the case of the PTR, they have now complicated their qualification process by asking prospective coaches to select which type of player they want to work with. The categories are: 10 and under; 11 to 17; Performance; or Adult Development. The coaches will then choose to attend one of these specific training courses for four days, with the exam on the fifth day. If successful, they are then qualified to go out and coach at the more specialised level, but, in theory of course, only dealing with those in the category they have received training for.

But why create such complications by introducing choices that are frankly unnecessary and, into the bargain, mean that coaches have to fork out yet more money in order to coach in more than one category?

Whether the beginner is ten years old or fifty years old, all he wants to learn is how to get the ball over the net like a proper tennis player – the techniques he needs to be given are just the same. The coach, therefore, will use the same knowledge to teach him, no matter what his age. He may well, of course, approach the lessons slightly differently, depending on the ability, aptitude, personality, etc. of the pupil, but, essentially, he will be teaching the same basics to everybody.

Unlike the PTR, however, the Spanish and European RPT have been persuaded, with respect to their operations in the UK, to follow similar lines to those of the LTA coaching structure. The RPT now incorporate a Level 1 and Level 2 which you must first pass before taking Level 3, which is when you actually qualify as a coach. But, just as in the LTA coaching structure, having successfully completed Levels 1 and 2, you are still only an assistant, and are not allowed to teach on your own.

Such complications that have built up over the years have led me to conclude that the whole coaching system in Britain is a mess, and quite frankly needs a major overhaul. However, as already alluded to with all the updating, you have to delve below the surface in order to appreciate what is really going on.

All three coaching organisations have very professional-looking websites and regularly produce the glossiest of brochures, giving the impression that everything is absolutely first-class, with wonderfully knowledgeable and superbly trained coaches. Nothing could be further from the truth. The more you read of this book, the more you will come to realise what I am getting at.

To explain – and delve – a little more, and also to risk confusing you, I set out the following:

According to the LTA system, at the time of writing, as one cannot be sure as to when it will change again, you can train to be a Coaching Assistant (Level 1), a Coaching Assistant (Level 2), a Coach (C) (Level 3), a Senior Club Coach (SCC) (Level 4), a Senior Performance Coach (SPC) (Level 4), a Master Club Coach (MCC) (Level 5), or a Master Performance Coach (MPC) (Level 5).

The caveat to the above is that this coaching structure has been recently updated, and, because the structure is updated, or changed, tweaked, reformed, reorganised... so regularly, an explanation is needed to clarify the qualifications of coaches who trained under a previous system and were given different titles. In order not to bore you, I shall leave this out. It can, of course, be checked on the LTA website, but, be warned, it is complicated.

Moreover, for the later qualification stages, coaches

select which qualification path they wish to follow, based on their playing standard. Whether the general public, perhaps looking for a suitable coach, are going to understand this further differentiation is very much open to question. In any case, I should point out that this extra grading, based upon playing standard, was tried by another coaching organisation in recent times, but was not at all popular, and was abandoned very quickly.

It is worth noting that these constant changes over the years to the qualification system and the courses on offer, in name, content, duration and cost, have not always been welcomed with open arms by the coaches. An instance of this was when they changed the old Part 1, 2, and 3 to Elementary, Intermediate and Professional, and then someone from the Coaching Department decided to rename the Intermediate title and call it Assistant.

There was absolute uproar from the newly-qualified Intermediate coaches who were henceforth now going to be known as Coach Assistants, giving the impression that they were only fit to teach under the supervision of a fully-qualified coach; it also made them look as though they were not even as qualified as the Elementary coaches, most of whom were only teaching tennis as a hobby while working full-time at something else.

This is a very good example of how somebody in power at the LTA decides to make a change and introduce something new, when the idea has not been properly thought through. It also reveals a lack of awareness of how things are on the ground, i.e. reality. Needless to say, the idea of Coach Assistant died a very swift death, and a different title had to be thought up, with yet more title changes made shortly afterwards.

To complicate matters even further, among the almost 4,000 LTA-qualified coaches in the UK, there are two categories: Registered or Licensed. If you are the former, you are probably a hobby or part-time coach and do not have to attend extra courses, but, if you are the latter, usually full-time, you have to go on what are called Accreditation Courses to keep your licence. This involves spending about two and a half days a year on courses, which have to be paid for by the coach, in order to obtain the right number of credits to be able to carry on coaching with the full backing of the LTA.

Impressively, Accreditation Courses are described as 'Continuous Professional Development' (CPD), involving 'a rolling programme of one-day courses covering specific and relevant topics'. And there are hundreds of them.

To an outsider, like Patrice Hagueleur, the Frenchman mentioned earlier, brought in to sort out British tennis, or the American journalist of Chapter 4, all these qualifications and courses must have appeared most impressive on paper, but the reality is quite different because the content, or core, as I have said already, is nowhere near sound enough to train coaches properly.

Generally the subject matter of the courses is interesting enough, but is rarely relevant to what customers learning to play tennis really need. The coach therefore is not equipped to teach his pupils what they have come for.

In Chapter 11 'Coaching', you will find countless examples of the consequences of such poor training.

As stated before in Chapter 1, when I described my great dissatisfaction with the LTA course I went on, what I found then, i.e. the complete lack of precision and method on the technical side, still persists on the main LTA qualification courses.

References to the 'shape' of the stroke, or 'long swing planes', are not adequate when teaching trainee coaches, or pupils who are just starting out, about how exactly sound strokes are produced.

And when we come to the extra Accreditation Courses (Continuous Professional Development), usually on other aspects of tennis, it seems to be pot luck as to whether a licensed coach finds such a course to be useful or a waste of time.

One coach told me he had been subjected to, and supremely bored by, a course about 'The Flight of the Ball', adding that he would have much preferred 'The Flight of the Bumble Bee' and his money back.

Another coach, however, informed me that he had found his course very enlightening about how very advanced players move on the court so as to recover their position incredibly quickly.

Since these courses are compulsory, forming part of the Coaching Qualification Pathway, and have to be paid for by the coaches, they should at least be relevant at all times, as the LTA claim they are, and, if possible, inspiring, but there is no guarantee that they will be either.

Far more serious, though, than a few extra courses that are sometimes boring, and even irrelevant, is the fact that it is so difficult, from my vantage point, to find a coach who can run a group session effectively, who knows thoroughly the basics of tennis and what to look for when coaching or rallying with a pupil, and who knows what to teach and in what order, so that the learner can quickly become a competent tennis player.

Over the years, when asking many coaches how they might start teaching a class of ten year-old beginners to play,

I have hoped against hope that they might come up with the idea of a logical system for learning from scratch, in order to give me the confidence to employ them. Unfortunately, out of all the answers I have heard, a system has never been mentioned.

'It depends,' is a very common response, and from my extensive experience of seeing coaching at grass-roots level, it would seem that 'it depends' refers more to how the coach is feeling at the time, rather than having the discipline or knowledge to follow a step-by-step approach to the teaching of tennis.

How can anyone learn to rally with good technique and develop as a player, which, after all, is the reason he has come for lessons in the first place, if the coach is so haphazard in the way he goes about things?

I do, though, understand why coaches are so nebulous and vague in their answers because, after gaining my first LTA qualification, I was in exactly the same position.

To illustrate further what I mean: on one occasion I asked a coach who wanted to work at my academy how he would go about teaching a class of young beginners. The usual 'it depends' came as the first response, but I insisted on an answer, repeating that they were complete beginners. After thinking for a few moments, he said he would teach them ABC. He then explained that ABC meant Agility, Balance and Coordination. I was, in fact, well aware of what he was referring to, but my opinion of ABC is that, while exercises can be given to improve a player's Agility, etc., it cannot actually be taught. I therefore wondered quietly to myself how and why anyone would try to teach ABC, considering that we are all born with a certain amount of agility, balance and coordination anyway, and youngsters attending coaching want nothing more than to learn the basics of tennis.

I decided, however, to accept his answer that he would spend the first few lessons teaching ABC. I then asked him what he would coach next, after ABC. Following a short pause, he replied: 'More ABC'!

I did not offer him the job, although I did have some sympathy for him because his obsession with ABC was not his fault – it was the way he had been trained: ABC is taught on a number of LTA Accreditation Courses as part of a coach's Continuous Professional Development.

I ask again: how can we in Great Britain achieve anything at grass-roots level if the LTA allow coaches to qualify with no real idea of what to teach, or how to teach, our beginners, and even how to conduct a group lesson properly?

At this juncture, you, the reader, may well think, or even protest, that it cannot be as bad as this all over the country, and I have to admit I do not honestly know because I have not carried out a proper nationwide survey, but, whenever I happen to observe a coaching session on my travels, I always see the same 'fun' approach to the exclusion of almost everything else. No technical teaching, no real progress being made, and often all carried out by an LTA-licensed Head Coach in a club that is Clubmarked – i.e. highly rated by the LTA.

No wonder I have had youngsters come to my academy, having started with other coaches, saying, with relief and gratitude, that they were at last learning to hit a tennis ball properly with me, and did not have to put up with silly games all the time, and meaningless waffle.

I may not be absolutely sure about the situation with coaching at grass-roots level in the whole of the UK, but what I do know is that during the last decade some forty to fifty LTA coaches have come to me for advice and training because they have realised that they do not know nearly enough about how to conduct a lesson effectively, or how to teach the basic strokes, and they have all left me saying that I have given them much-needed confidence and knowledge about how to coach properly. My co-author is telling me to add a little more, so I shall. In fact, they are generally amazed at how differently I approach coaching, and usually ask where I learnt it all. No one has ever voiced disapproval of my system and the methods I use – on the contrary, they have completely embraced what I have shown them.

It goes without saying that coaches need good support in the form of clear and precise advice and training, but, quite frankly, they are not getting it.

For my own guidance, and that of my assistants, I compiled a manual on how to conduct a group lesson, how to teach the techniques for the eight most important strokes in the game, and a logical order for coaches to follow. It contains very basic, but extremely important, steps on how to proceed. It is astonishing that, with regard to supervising a group, none of the key points has ever been covered in any course I have been on – and I have been on so many. What I have put in the manual is simple, down-to-earth advice on how to handle and teach groups of juniors so that they receive the best possible lesson every time.

In my opinion, what is in my manual should be taught to all coaches as part of their training. At the moment, it seems that they are just left to work it out for themselves, which some do eventually, with varying degrees of success, or they simply end up muddling through as best they can. Perhaps because I am so near to reality, the very practical step-by-step advice I give has just not been thought of by those at the LTA.

It has to be said that the great enthusiasm many coaches have for the job could be harnessed so much better with more thorough training: the knock-on effect would be tremendous for our juniors and other beginners, giving them the opportunity to reach their full potential, and even turning the more talented among them into world-class, or, at least, it would give them the chance to get very near it – something that definitely does not happen now.

In 2013 a number of coaches complained that the website created for them by the LTA was too 'complicated' and that communications were 'sporadic and often irrelevant'. Such a highly unsatisfactory state of affairs had come about despite all the qualifications and plethora of courses available. As has been said before, when systems and structures are constantly changed (the NHS ... Education...), the implication is that those in charge do not really know what to do to get it right, so they tweak, reorganise, reform and update, and everything is turned into more and more of a mess.

I have even come to realise that the more coaches are taught, the more confused they seem to get. But this is perfectly understandable when they do not have a system to follow in the first place, or a proper understanding of the technical elements which make up all the strokes in the game. It is little wonder, therefore, that coaches, coming off the accreditation courses they have to attend, do not know where their new knowledge fits in.

Their brains are simply filled with a jumble of coaching information which they call upon randomly, according to how they feel on the day. I have had top coaches admit to me that they know nothing about technique, so they keep their juniors running furiously around with drills and little fun games.

And many have also told me that, having attended a lecture on one particular aspect of the game, they then teach this to all and sundry for the following week, whether it is relevant for their pupils or not. They then feel good about themselves because the knowledge they have just acquired gives them something new to teach for a change.

So the bad coaching goes on, with virtually everyone brainwashed into thinking that fun is the be-all and end-all. Vague instructions, catchphrases and buzzwords suffice for the technical side. Keep them moving, do a few drills, play some fun games, crack lots of jokes and end with a mini competition, announcing that nobody has lost, they just 'came second'.

If there is any attempt at technical instruction, the coach will do it by telling the juniors to swing from low to high for their topspin groundstrokes, and will get them serving after one exercise of throwing a ball down the court before trying the real thing with a racquet.

The coach thinks he has done a good job – it was the way he was taught anyway as a youngster, and was confirmed as the right way to coach on his LTA qualification course –the parents are happy because their eight year-old Johnny is out of breath, smiling from the fun of it all, and has hit loads of balls, with no correction of bad technique, of course, but the parents do not realise that. Lesson after lesson with no real learning or progress. It is extremely fortunate for the LTA that there are no Ofsted inspectors for tennis classes in this country!

And the situation is just the same a year or two down the line, when the juniors have got a bit better, with training at county, or, as it is now, at regional level: youngsters being taught by coaches doing the same old drills that they did as juniors themselves, with hardly any technical input, except for the latest encouraging buzzword which teaches nothing, and actually shows that the coach is completely ignorant of the elements that go to make up a sound stroke. In effect, failures teaching the next generation to fail. Just hit loads of balls and eventually you will get it right.

Of course, with clear and precise technical coaching, the player would get it right immediately, and, if it started to go wrong, the attentive and well-trained coach would correct it and keep the player on the right path.

In golf, this is exactly what happens, and is the reason the leaderboards in top tournaments often show the following: GB and Northern Ireland unless stated.

The simple fact is – there are British world-class golfers in abundance. Our young professionals make the grade because they were given sound fundamentals to start with and were never allowed to stray.

Coming away now from the woes of coaching in Great Britain and returning to the 2006 Blueprint or Action Plan, we find the following statement: 'Community tennis (has been) neglected over the last 20 years' and there will be 'cohesive support (for) schools ... parks ... tennis centres'.

My co-author remembers clearly the disparaging remarks about park players made to him by a top LTA coach some forty years ago: 'They all have frying pan handle grips (for serving), crude and ugly strokes, and would never be allowed into a proper club.'

The idea, however, of trying to make tennis less elitist has been around for some time: the Cliff Richard Tennis Foundation was set up in the early 1990s – the 'Search for a Star', for example, mentioned in Chapter 1, later becoming known as simply the Tennis Foundation – a charity whose aim is to engage with all parts of the community, recognising diversity and promoting inclusion; it is now the country's largest tennis charity, working in partnership with the LTA, and had Sue Mappin, the ex-professional tennis player, as its Executive Director until 2010.

In addition to this, there is the very successful Tennis for Free (TFF) campaign, started up in 2003 by Tony Hawks, a comedian with a serious passion for the sport and a great believer in providing free tennis facilities in parks for absolutely everybody, with regular free coaching as well.

It is ironic that what he pleaded for in his tussles with the LTA a number of years ago has finally found favour, with the grass roots now definitely at the top of the agenda, and massive initiatives being organised to offer free tennis sessions in parks all over the country. The money has certainly been made available, but, whether it is from some of the Wimbledon profits, as Tony Hawks suggested it should be, or from the Tennis Foundation and Sport England funding, is not clear.

In order to provide the 'cohesive support' for community tennis, it has to be said anyway that the LTA have put in a considerable effort since 2006 and spent mouth-watering sums of money. In 2012, the LTA and the Tennis Foundation charity jointly invested £73.2m in grass-roots tennis in the UK. That is double what the LTA receive through the Wimbledon profits each year, which in itself is considered colossal.

Also, in 2009, as mentioned before, the life assurance and pensions company, Aegon UK, signed a deal with the LTA to invest in grass-roots and schools tennis that will effectively go through to 2017.

Free introductions to the sport, in the form of Cardio tennis and mini tennis for young children, with equipment provided and coaches or instructors laid on, have been the order of the day in parks, schools, and community tennis centres.

Websites are on hand to 'Find a place to play', 'All Play Tennis', 'Find a player', and 'Find a coach', and many adverts have been placed in the press, urging people to give tennis a try.

However, as already stated previously, the upshot of all these very costly efforts has been that the numbers playing tennis have actually gone down, leading to Sport England withholding £10.3m of funding in December, 2012, and the Chair of the All-Party Tennis Group in the House of Lords, Baroness Billingham, describing the LTA as 'useless'.

All this bad press was followed by a whirlwind of frenzied activity at the LTA throughout 2013, with even more adverts being placed in the press, both national and local, extolling the virtues of this fun game called tennis, and Roger Draper speaking to the media at the beginning of the Wimbledon fortnight telling everybody who did not play to give it a go by turning up for Cardio tennis in local parks and community centres, where there would be free sessions with all equipment provided. It would be a fun day for the family, he said, great for fitness – just give the ball a whack, no technique required.

It should be explained that Cardio tennis uses low compression balls, so, if you give them a 'whack', they will not fly into the nearby cafe, and the instructors are often non-tennis players who have been on a day's course to learn how to deliver the one-hour session. It is basically aerobics on a tennis court, with up-tempo music to add to the atmosphere. It is certainly fun and good for fitness, and is more attractive for some than going to the gym.

However, if you want to know, out of curiosity, or real keenness, how to grip the racquet for a backhand, as opposed to a forehand, or anything else about tennis, it will be no good asking the instructor. Actually to learn about the sport, as played by more experienced aficionados, you would have to be inspired, and directed, to join a group learning the full version with a coach.

Since the numbers playing tennis at least once a week for half an hour or more have gone down in recent years, one might well question the effectiveness of all these initiatives. In the next chapter entitled 'Schools', there is more comment on the LTA's attempts to increase participation in the sport.

And even if these massive initiatives to take tennis beyond the middle classes led to a huge increase in participation, the outcome would still be disappointing because of the ineffective coaching we have in Great Britain. You have had a glimpse of it in this chapter, but just wait until you get to the chapter on coaching.

Tony Hawks and his team have certainly done a very good job in working with borough councils to make park courts free, etc., just as they are in the USA, so now, in order to play, or learn to play, you do not have to join an expensive, stuffy and socially cliquey club, as he puts it, where, incredibly, you might still have to wear predominantly white clothing – even today it is the rule that prevails for adults and juniors at my local tennis club.

'Tennis in the park' then, does seem, on the surface, to have a very promising ring about it: after all, Serena and Venus Williams learnt to play superbly in such circumstances, but, it has to be remembered, they were under the sole guidance of their father who had the wisdom to keep them away from the stress of junior tournaments, and allowed them to develop unhindered as free spirits, while he consulted coaching manuals so that he could teach them the strokes of the game.

For the two sisters it was the equivalent, in educational terms, of being in a state school with no contact at all with the ordinary teachers, except for one private tutor who gave them his undivided attention. In effect, they had very special and elitist treatment, albeit in humble and grass-roots surroundings.

Not quite the same here in the Tony Hawks set-up, although, with proper coaching and guidance, the scheme could indeed see some good results. It is ironic that, twenty years ago, there were 33,000 park courts in the UK, and, in 2008, with so much more activity going on, there were only 10,000.

After Andy Murray won Wimbledon in 2013, his mother, Judy, said that the infrastructure for tennis was lacking in Great Britain: there are great swathes of the country where you cannot find a tennis court for miles and miles, so how can youngsters, inspired by her son, 'find a place to play' in such areas?

The solution might be to build loads more tennis courts, as in France, for example, where virtually every village, however small, has two or more public courts for anyone to use. They are well maintained and can usually be accessed by going to a local shop to get the key on payment of a few Euros. There are always notices on the courts giving information about how to hire them, and also about the once- or twice-weekly visits of a coach.

This could certainly work here, the LTA still have a lot of money, despite recent cutbacks, and could undertake the building of the courts, but the one problem for us would be: could the roaming grass-roots coach teach properly, or just entertain? Certainly, in France, the former applies rather than the latter, judging by the number of French players in the top 100, or even top 50.

When Roger Draper took over as the Chief Executive Officer in 2006, he must have thought that it was quite in order to leave the Coaching Department alone – so impressed must he have been with the hundreds of courses available for coaches, all the constantly updated qualifications on offer, from learning how to teach mini tennis to six year-olds right up to how to deal with top performance players, and also how to manage clubs and teams of coaches, etc.; moreover, he would have seen beautifully presented Training Programmes, carefully worked out for different age groups, with comprehensive guidelines on to how to develop a player from a very young age right up to twenty and beyond, and so on, and so on. However, in 2013, he is reported to have said that he wished he had looked more carefully at coaching. Had he done so, this book might never have been written.

If Mr. Draper ignored the Coaching Department, he certainly was not slow in turning his attention to other areas, and, in the opinion of many, succeeded in transforming the creaking and unwieldy infrastructure of the old LTA into something much more streamlined and up-to-date – although there are still those who maintain that the organisation continues to be weighed down by excessive bureaucracy.

As evidence of at least some improvement, the LTA gained a two-star 'outstanding' rating in the Best Companies Accreditation 2012 Survey. The quality of Roger Draper's work on the commercial and business side cannot be questioned, it seems, and, if he had achieved anything like success on the elite performance side by starting to bring players through towards the top of the sport, he would have probably still been at the helm in 2016, the end of the ten-year Action Plan or Blueprint, and might even have been invited to stay on.

However, all is not what it seems when one deals with the LTA, and it is difficult to know what is really going on behind the expensive and impressive gates of the National Tennis Centre in Roehampton.

Despite all the much-vaunted restructuring and modernising that had taken place, there was a sudden exodus in 2009 of a number of top people from the LTA 'for personal reasons': Carl Maes, the Head of Women's Tennis, went back to Belgium; Paul Hutchins, the Head of Men's Tennis, departed; likewise the Head of Coach Support, the Finance Director, and one of the key Strength and Conditioning Coaches; and the Head of Sports Science went back to her native Australia, never to return because of 'visa problems'.

Secrecy surrounded the whole affair, and Jonathan Overend, the BBC tennis correspondent at the time, was prompted to write a blog entitled *Who wants to work for British tennis?* (April, 2009). An insider called the situation a 'chaotic mess', and the Daily Mail described the LTA as 'super dysfunctional'.

In the same year, as reported in The Telegraph newspaper on 23rd February 2009, Anne Keothavong thanked the Belgian, Carl Maes, and other coaches, for helping her reach the top 50 in the world, but, at the same time, referred to 'unprofessional people' at the LTA hindering her progress in the past, adding that she was of the opinion that there were still 'unprofessional people' working in the organisation. Would this be the 'dead wood' of previous regimes, much commented on over the decades in tennis circles around the country, or would she even be referring to poorly-trained British coaches?

A year later, another well-known figure mysteriously packed her bags – Sue Mappin, the respected Executive Director of the LTA-controlled Charity, the Tennis Foundation. Her commitment to, and work in, promoting parks and schools tennis were much admired, and disgruntled community club members demanded a meeting with the trustees of the Foundation to find out why she had left. No reason was forthcoming – just a curt statement emerged from the LTA: 'We do not discuss individual contracts'.

An article in the Daily Mail on the 18th August, 2010, made reference to the LTA's 'long history of poor staff management'. There were also comments in the press generally about big salaries and big pay-offs, which brought the following reaction: 'We do not discuss the remuneration of LTA staff, nor are we under any obligation to do so'.

This book is about the reality of British tennis, but, as can be seen from the above, reality is in short supply when it comes to the governing body, it seems. A Chief Executive Officer with great business and commercial skills, and yet we hear of an alleged chaotic mess within. So what was really going on? The LTA 'cannot retain key staff because of disenchantment' (Daily Mail, 18th August, 2010), and yet the CEO talks in an interview about how they all 'continually work' on improving the way they communicate, and spend a lot of 'time on colleague engagement and work and well-being' (GlobalSportsJobs, 15th November, 2012).

It is worth pointing out that Roger Draper refused five times between 2006-2010, to talk about the state of British tennis on TV with the Sky Sports presenter and commentator, Mark Petchey. Why be afraid of discussing what is really going on, and why not show a willingness to communicate and explain? This, I believe, is what politicians call transparency, and it can be extremely effective if properly applied, and not just bandied around as a buzzword – which tends to happen in politics. Indeed, transparency is not unknown to the LTA: it certainly happens now with regard to the funding of promising players, so why not extend it and engage with those who want to know what is really going on?

Perhaps the problem stems from the tone of the 2006 Blueprint. As an Action Plan it would pass an Ofsted inspection with flying colours – in terms of paperwork, it is most impressive. It was published after much consultation, and could not be more wide-ranging and thorough in its analysis of the situation, with objectives and goals clearly set out. However, turning it all into reality has been another matter entirely.

Interestingly, it uses a certain type of language: it states that the NTC research and development centre at Roehampton will be 'the hub for British tennis' – 'a hive of tennis activity with players and coaches visiting to learn and gain experience from working with each other and some of the world's best tennis people'; it will provide 'an unrivalled experience'.

In reality, the NTC (National Tennis Centre) has been described by many as a 'white elephant', and the atmosphere therein as sterile and far from stimulating; Andy Murray has said that, when he visits, there is hardly anybody there.

Performance Centres, with 'high quality programmes particularly for younger players', will be 'hives of talent development' and 'feeders' for top clubs and centres. 'About' 175 Performance Centres, 'about' forty to fifty High Performance Centres, and 'up to' ten International Performance Centres are envisaged. In reality, at the time of writing, there are seventy-two Performance Centres, seventeen High, and four International. You will read later my observations on what goes on in some Performance Centres.

In the community – schools and parks – there will be coaches of the right quality to get people playing the game 'fast!'. 'They will become the 'pied pipers of tennis'. I refer you to the rest of the book for a reality check.

Three 'Drivers' will 'create a climate of success and a culture with winning at the heart of everything we do, from community, schools and parks to clubs and all the way through to centre court'.

The Blueprint finishes with: 'These are our ideas and proposals for the direction of British tennis going forward'.

The language, as can be seen, is idealistic and somewhat pretentious, even naive – e.g. '...through to centre court' ... 'pied pipers'. It is also corporate in tone – the sort of language you find in the business plans of big companies: '...the direction of British tennis going forward'. How else could it go – backwards, sideways?; 'hive(s)'; 'hub'; 'drivers' – all sounding very impressive, but what about reality, and what is actually happening?

And then we have the language as spoken by LTA executives when dealing with the media, and even with each other – the mind boggleth. On 15th November, 2012, after the LTA had been awarded a two-star 'outstanding' rating in the Best Companies Accreditation Survey, in the interview already referred to in GlobalSportsJobs, a digital media platform for the international sports industry, Roger Draper said that, if anyone wanted to work for the LTA, they would have to bear in mind the following: 'We are all about making progress at a blistering pace that will always be challenging and demanding'.

A few months later, and true to form, as if he were reading a script from a corporate text book, Mr. Draper described the renewal until 2017 of the 'Lead Partner' deal with Aegon UK, supporting British tennis, as 'groundbreaking' and as 'taking it to a new level'. The announcement was made in great style in a video that was posted on the LTA website.

In an article that appeared on a BBC website in January, 2013, the LTA, as if quoting verbatim from a report destined for a Parliamentary Committee, stated that they were 'looking forward to implementing the final phase' of their 10-year plan for the game, a plan that was 'a well-articulated road map' about how to transform the sport and the organisation. They concluded by saying that they were in a position where they could 'proactively look to the next phase of really engaging with players and fans – from the ages of three to 83 – up and down the country'. They were 'in good shape but in no way complacent'.

It is of relevance here to point out that this article was published very soon after the stinging criticism in December, 2012, regarding grass-roots tennis, from Sport England and the House of Lords All-Party Tennis Group, chaired by Baroness Billingham.

Bearing this in mind, the LTA refer to their 'drive to increase grass-roots participation' as a 'quest given extra focus by demands from ... Sport England', and that it (Sport England) 'may reduce the amount of cash for tennis that it allocates' to them. There is no mention of the fact that Sport England have already withheld £10.3m of funding and have threatened to find someone else to do the job of increasing the numbers playing tennis if they (the LTA) continue to fail. Baroness Billingham's comment that they are 'useless' is not mentioned either, understandably perhaps, just: 'We realise we haven't got everything right. But it is a very competitive (leisure) marketplace.'

In order to boost their image and create a feel-good factor they also use incredibly optimistic language in the article, but whether it is based on reality, or realistic analysis, is open to question. They boldly state: 'We are lucky to be on the cusp of a golden era of British tennis'.

The 2006 Blueprint shows similar optimism, but possibly more long-term, when it states that the 'new vision' is for 'British tennis players winning Slams, ATP, WTA, ITF and Tennis Europe Tournaments and, ultimately, the Davis Cup and Federation Cup'.

They are also good at quoting statistics along the lines of: 'More than 2 million children have access to tennis at school'. It sounds so wonderful, but may I proactively invite you to see what this really means in the next chapter on schools?

In addition, statistics are massaged to great effect as well. In the article we are informed that in 2006 Great Britain had two players in the top 100. This appears in the Blueprint and refers to singles rankings; in 2013, we are told, there are ten in the top 100, but the criteria have been changed by including doubles players. Here the LTA are doing exactly what they did in 2010, the year of the Davis Cup débâcle against Lithuania, in order to impress the Parliamentary Watchdog investigating their poor reputation and results. They were, at the time, rebuked for their 'confusing replies'. What they should have said in the article is that there were three British players in the top 100 in January, 2013 – an increase of one compared to 2006.

Again, reality does not count.

In an updated version doubles has been added to the 2013 statistic, whereas it was missing in the original. It has also been put under the heading of 'LTA Tennis Facts and Figures' in order to highlight such an impressive piece of information, rather than just being mentioned in the main text.

However, it is still very misleading and goes against the singles yardstick that is used by all tennis federations when they refer to their success, or lack of it, in the world game. It would be interesting to ask someone in authority at the LTA the following: what happens if a player has a top 100 ranking in both singles and doubles? Is he to be counted twice?

It is also relevant here to point out that doubles specialists who play no singles at all have to be very much in the upper reaches of the top 100 in order to earn the sort of money that befits a high-level sportsman. Moreover, doubles is very different from singles and does not require nearly as much skill or fitness: the rallies are much shorter, with the construction of points less demanding, and most players who become doubles specialists do so because they only have to compete against others who are not technically proficient enough, or confident enough, to make it in singles. Doubles is often referred to as a 'one-hit wonder' format, because that is exactly what it is, and so suits the British approach to tennis, with consistent baseline rallying and the building of a point rarely required.

To the casual reader the article on the BBC website would appear to reflect not too badly on the LTA – such is the power of language and the way things are presented: it is only when one delves into the background of what is said, and the reality that has prompted its publication, that one becomes aware that it is all very much about image-boosting and public relations.

Even when a much-needed improvement has successfully been made and has become part of reality as we know it, the temptation to dress it up in impressive language cannot be resisted. Before 2006 the funding of promising players – how decisions were made, how much a player received, etc. – gave rise to a lot of controversy and dissatisfaction. Funding is now much more clear, fair and transparent, and can be checked out on the relevant LTA website.

It is also backed up by a Talent Identification system at county, regional and national level, although, whether it reaches out to the Tennis For Free activities in parks, I do not know.

In liaison with local coaches, the Talent Team are on the lookout for promising players even if they are only seven years old, and some funding is available, in exceptional circumstances, from the age of eight. However, it is not just called 'Funding', but 'Matrix Funding'. Very impressive, n'est-ce pas?, and, if you do not know what 'matrix' means, it is possibly even more impressive, since it suggests special qualities about the clever people who came up with the word in the first place. I repeat, the set-up IS very comprehensive, and well explained on the website, but the choice of 'matrix' reveals a certain type of mindset: plain English is simply not good enough when you have a marketing mentality and are out to impress.

Similarly, not only does the language of the LTA often take us away from reality – it also denies reality. In the aforementioned article on the BBC website there appears the following statement:

'Some may incorrectly see tennis as a middle-class sport'. I think most people would change the word 'incorrectly' to 'correctly'. If you go down any inner-city high street and ask the passers-by how they view tennis, I am sure the replies would contradict such a statement time and time again.

A veritable sea change in British society and way of life would be necessary to alter this state of affairs. 'Wimbledon is a celebration of the British middle classes – it is part of their summer season,' said Tony Hawks (Tennis For Free), and he was not far wrong.

The 2006 Blueprint concedes that 'tennis is expensive', but, despite this, reality-denying assertions are still made by the LTA, in this case to the effect that it only costs £1.50 a week for a junior to play at a club. This may well be so, in some clubs in Great Britain when he is just starting out, but 'tennis is a very technical sport', as the Talent ID website puts it, and early coaching is essential in order to make progress – this means, quite simply, that extra money has to be found.

In addition, commercial centres with indoor courts often exclude juniors, unless their parents join as well and pay the very high membership fees. It is true that, at some centres, mini tennis is available for non-members, but it then costs more per hour than for members. Whatever the status of the youngster, though, the price for hourly mini tennis is way, way above the '£1.50p a week' quoted by the LTA.

One can understand why Tony Hawks started up his TFF (Tennis For Free) in local parks in 2003: at least he was more aware of reality than the LTA.

After Wimbledon 2013, Roger Draper said that success does not depend on coming from a privileged and wealthy area of the country with a tradition in tennis: he pointed out that Andy Murray is from Dunblane, in Scotland, which was not at all known for its tennis a few years ago.

However, what he omitted to say was that Andy has a tennis-connected mother who became a full-time coach when he was aged nine; she also played competitively when she was younger before turning to coaching. She therefore knew how to guide him and his brother, Jamie, way before they even reached their teens. There was also enough money at hand, presumably, to send Andy to Spain at the age of fifteen and Jamie to an independent school in Cambridge with facilities for training from LTA coaches.

'I am ensuring that the children on my course are growing with the sport'; 'my assistant and I are getting them to develop their skills'. Even LTA coaches are not exempt from using set phrases that sound impressive but do not stand up to analysis.

This particular person was a young Head Coach, fully-qualified and licensed, delivering an eight-day course in 2013 at a 'clubmarked' club – i.e. highly rated, according to strict criteria, by the LTA. When asked how exactly he was ensuring that the children were 'growing with the sport' and 'developing their skills', he could not answer, and even considered the question provocatively difficult.

Once again I make reference to the same quotation from the LTA Talent ID website with no apologies for repeating it: 'Tennis is a very technical sport', so why was he, a Head Coach, incapable of coming up with an answer? It is commonly accepted that coaches are able to teach technique, but not in his case, apparently.

It is also commonly accepted that a coach should be organised: his assistant had taken the course for the first four days, but he, the Head Coach, had not liaised with him to find out what exactly had been covered during that time. There was therefore no chance of continuity and a sense of progress for the pupils.

Catchphrases and buzzwords that taught nothing, coupled with shouts of encouragement – 'white noise' – could constantly be heard during the lesson. The coach was doing what he had been taught on an LTA course, but the children looked bored because the stimulation of actually learning something was missing. As one would expect, the de rigueur word just had to come out to round off the fine-sounding set phrases: he said he was making sure they all had a 'fun time'. In case you have not been paying attention, the de rigueur word is FUN.

This chapter could have been called 'Appearance ... Reality ... and the LTA', and might easily have turned into a huge tome worthy of a PhD thesis. I, for one, am happy that it did not, and I expect that you, the reader, are even happier.

It has already taken up many pages – perhaps too many – but I can assure you that it would have occupied even more space had I chosen to describe in detail other aspects of this 'Background to the Mess'. Some examples in résumé form would be: the constant procession of Chief Executive Officers coming and going over the decades, all bringing great hopes of success and all ending in failure; the practice of setting highly ambitious targets, this time in 2006, only for them to be modified a couple of years later, and still not met at the time of writing; media rumours about the Aegon UK 'Lead Partner' deal (2009-2017) being worth much less than publicised after consultants, agents and hospitality had been paid for; and so on, and so on...

Make it look good, make it sound good, tell people you are working at 'a blistering pace', change the names of a few titles to suggest improvements have been made with 'no stone unturned', to quote another overused cliché that is designed to impress, spend millions on this and millions on that, come up with mind-boggling statistics that often mislead, announce that 'the foundations are now in place ... (including) an incredibly strong board and governance structure', assure everybody that we are 'on the cusp of a golden era' and that tennis is being established as 'a game for everyone', and you are sure to convince the world that you are doing a grand job, and you will even believe it too, such is the power of language and hard work.

Unfortunately, I, for one, am getting tired of hearing it – maybe you are, as well. It has been said that the splendour of Wimbledon has hidden the decline of British tennis for many years, and still does, despite Andy Murray, but the splendour of the LTA's language can no longer be allowed to hide the reality of the sport in the UK.

This book is about that reality.

May I now refer you to the next chapter which has relevance to the mess we are in, but also, importantly, it takes us closer to the solution.

CHAPTER 6

Schools

Since this book is about the reality of British tennis and how to solve the mess contained therein, a chapter has to be included on what is happening, and has been happening, with regard to the teaching of the sport in our schools. After all, most youngsters will have their first experience of tennis at school, unless their parents are regular players, in which case they may well be introduced to the game before they even go to school. Moreover, the LTA have been very active in promoting schools tennis for a number of years, and not just since the 2006 Blueprint and the advent of Aegon money in 2009.

And still on the theme of reality: if you do not start at a very young age in tennis, you have virtually no chance of making it professionally. The American, Jennifer Capriati, won the French and US Open junior titles before her thirteenth birthday, having received her first tennis lesson at the age of three; Steffi Graf won the German under-18 title when she was just thirteen, having started at the age of three with a cut-down wooden racquet, and spending hours and hours practising with her father; the Swiss player, Martina Hingis, won a Grand Slam at just fifteen years of age, and was reportedly playing when she was only two; Laura Robson won junior Wimbledon when she was fourteen, and started playing 'as soon as she could hold a tennis racquet', according to her parents; Heather Watson was playing by the time she was seven, and Andy and Jamie Murray were on the tennis court by the age of five, if not before; the list could go on and on.

The conclusion is obvious: you have to get them playing as young as possible. There is even a case for starting at kindergarten level rather than primary. Certainly, most experts will have you believe that secondary school is too late for most children if they want to have a chance of being good enough to make a living out of the sport as professional players, although, from the point of view of increasing participation, introducing tennis to eleven and twelve year-olds should produce results.

My own personal belief, incidentally, is that a talented eleven year-old, starting tennis from scratch at secondary school, can still become world-class if given the correct guidance, but it is certainly true that a youngster of this age would have no time to lose, and would have three to four years of catching up to do, so starting before secondary school is definitely to be recommended.

There is a problem, however, with introducing tennis in primary schools and kindergartens: very few have proper facilities for the sport. This means that the PE teacher is faced with a large number of children in a very small area, such as an assembly hall, and has to use activities that cannot replicate the real thing.

Over the last decade or so, I have seen what happens in many primary schools: games are often organised that are unrelated to tennis – agility, balance and coordination can be a theme, for example, but the activity that challenges these skills is applicable to almost any sport; another much-used game can involve dribbling or rolling a ball along the ground using a racquet – more akin to hockey than tennis; and many games introduced to pupils, believing they are learning about the sport, are even played without ever touching a tennis racquet.

As a first experience of tennis, this cannot exactly be described as very positive or inspiring. If it were an introduction to golf or table tennis, the pupils would be learning how to hold and move the club or bat appropriately very soon after the start of their first lesson.

The same can be said for what happens with badminton: at the introductory stage, balloons are often used in place of shuttles, but the pupils are immediately using and swinging the racquet in a badminton way, and get a feel for the proper game.

For some reason, it just does not happen in tennis, when it should, and importantly could, if only the PE teachers were given better training.

As already quoted elsewhere, again, no apologies for repetition: 'Tennis is a very technical sport' (LTA Talent ID website).

And so is golf. If you asked a secondary school PE teacher to introduce golf to his pupils, he would probably baulk at the idea and would much prefer to send them to a qualified coach at a golf club, with proper practice facilities. Not being a golfer himself, and even if he were, he would be horrified at trying to explain the grip, posture, stance, ball position and basics of the golf swing, recognising that his pupils required technical coaching from day one. He simply would not want to pass on incorrect information and give the pupils bad habits.

Why is there not the same reaction when it comes to tennis? Both sports are very technical, and, yet, for some reason, it is considered quite acceptable for a PE teacher, usually with just three hours' LTA training and no specialist knowledge, to give young beginners their first taste of the sport.

Some of the early tennis experiences I have witnessed on many occasions in schools in the last two decades would certainly have driven me away from the sport as a pupil. It is little wonder that children with talent give up on tennis and choose something else, especially when, in the other activity, they can receive more relevant and realistic guidance from the word go, and they can relate what they are learning more directly to what they see the professionals doing on television.

I once observed, on the next court to me, how a PE teacher, fresh from his LTA 'coaching large groups in schools' course, asked the class to rally against a wall, and then proceeded to encourage each pupil in a loud voice: 'Come on, remember, Tim Henman! Tim Henman! Grand Slam points!'. This same instruction was repeated over and over again, despite none of the class having any control over the ball.

One of the girls directly asked the teacher how to do it properly, and all she got by way of coaching was: 'Just keep trying, and remember, Tim Henman!, Tim Henman! Grand Slam points!'.

In no way can this be described as a proper tennis lesson – in fact, it is decidedly off-putting for those involved, since they end up no wiser about the sport, and probably conclude that it is so difficult to play that they will steer well clear of it in the future.

When I later heard the 'Tim Henman, Tim Henman, Grand Slam points' cry from another PE teacher, I discovered they too had heard this coaching phrase on an

'LTA teaching large groups' course. Would there ever be a chance of hearing a piano teacher instruct his pupil, sitting in front of the keyboard for the first time, with the words: 'Just keep trying, and remember: Chopin!, Chopin!, Royal Festival Hall!'?

PE teachers will tell you that the plan for any sport in PE lessons is 'coach for the first half of the lesson, and get them playing in the second half'.

For most sports I am sure this will work. In rounders, for example, the first half of the lesson will probably comprise explaining something about positioning and the rules, and, with such little technical skill needing to be taught, in the second half of the lesson a rounders game can be successfully experienced by all. The same applies for football and netball, with finer skills and tactics slowly introduced week by week. Again, from the very first lesson these two sports can be played and enjoyed, and still with progress being made.

But in tennis, this approach of 'half the lesson – coach, half the lesson – play' most certainly does not work. How can anyone teach five basic strokes with the grip changes required, and give the necessary practice for these strokes, individually as well as combined, as is required in every rally, in less than several hours of coaching, let alone half a PE lesson?

As soon as pupils, fairly new to the game, start playing a match, there is hardly a rally to be enjoyed, with the ball out of control throughout. How frustrating and off-putting for any pupil who is really keen to understand and learn how to play properly.

When I visited a secondary school to give a two-hour professional tennis lesson to over sixty pupils on seven tennis courts, the PE teachers still had this 'the pupils must be allowed to play the game' mentality. The Head of PE brought out just 24 balls for me to use, thinking I did not need the other 100 balls he had left in the PE store. He was obviously thinking that the thirteen year-olds would be playing a doubles match, needing just two balls per court for the server. I assume as well that he was expecting me to shout instructions from the court side as they played a game.

If the PE teachers offer tennis at their school but do not know how to deliver a proper tennis lesson to a large group, and allow their pupils just to have a go, that is bad enough, but when they know a professional is arriving to coach, then they should realise that, if the pupils are still learning the fundamentals, which in this case they certainly were, then 150 balls would be the order of the day, and playing a proper game should simply not be on the agenda.

Several of the pupils thanked me quietly as they returned to their classrooms, with comments of how much they had enjoyed actually learning something for a change. They felt they had made real progress, and they had experienced tennis in a very different way. One pupil exclaimed: 'That was the best session of tennis I have ever had'. Not surprising, in the circumstances – it was probably the first time she had not been expected, and put under pressure, to play a proper match when she was nowhere near ready.

When I first had swimming lessons at school, I could not swim, but the PE teacher did not throw me into the deep end. Why does it have to be different in tennis?

Coaching properly has to be the right approach, and it is what juniors starting out in the sport actually want. Unfortunately, tennis, like golf, is not something that can be mastered within a few hours, so must be treated accordingly. This is why we have so many full-time tennis and golf coaches, whereas there are considerably fewer full-time coaches for most other sports.

It used to be 'Tim Henman! Tim Henman!', and now, a few years down the line, what we have from the LTA and the Tennis Foundation for teaching tennis in primary and secondary schools is just as ineffective, even with an 'innovative', pupil-facing DVD as an aid for the teacher.

The activities are similar and frankly do not teach tennis: children are shown trying to rally, with no technique, and are very bunched up, which is dangerous, with chaos, one feels, about to break out; there is still emphasis on rolling lots of balls; two people are seen attempting to keep a ball going across their own arms with a mini tennis racquet, while holding hands – an exercise of doubtful value and very doubtful duration; there is a lot of moving around by the pupils in the DVD, which looks good; much enthusiasm from the demonstrator, which sounds good, and, of course, everybody is having FUN. But it is not tennis coaching – indeed, some of what goes on will, in my opinion, only serve to instil bad habits and hinder anyone going on to play the game for real.

The DVD is supposed to show the class what to do and, therefore, allow the teacher to do what he does best – teach. Unfortunately, the teaching has very little to do with showing the pupils how to play tennis.

The only saving grace for this instructional schools' DVD is that, without model pupils, it would be impossible to conduct a class in such a controlled and safe manner, so any PE teacher would end up having to improvise anyway. I am therefore quite confident that the LTA lesson, as shown on the DVD, would never take place.

It is, however, portrayed as the way to coach a large group in a confined space, so again this brings into question the LTA's grasp of reality, and also their competence when it comes to coaching tennis.

As might be expected, the statistics provided by the LTA and the Tennis Foundation are most impressive, and even mind-boggling: more than 2 million children have had access to tennis at school; 400,000 racquets, 600,000 balls (or even 'nearly 800,000 balls', according to the Aegon Schools website – did the LTA miss a trick here?) have been provided free to primary schools; 15,000 teachers have received free tennis training. In the 'Written evidence submitted...' to the House of Commons Education Committee in March, 2013, this is expressed as support for 'more than 15,000 schools across Great Britain...the vast majority being state schools'; '26,000+ teachers and coaches' have been given training to help them deliver tennis in schools (from the same 'Written evidence...' to the Education Committee); 80% of all schools 'in England' now offer tennis (from another LTA source); 47% have a club link with local tennis centres – '... we encourage coaches and tennis venues to link to their local schools', (from 'Written evidence...' again); 'more than 46,000 pupils took part in a schools tennis competition' in 2012; and so on, and so on...

It all looks and sounds so good, just like the aforementioned 'innovative', pupil-facing DVD: at first glance, it seems fine. With such material, or similar, as evidence, no wonder the American journalist of Chapter 4 was satisfied with the efforts of the LTA Coaching Department and delved no further.

However, when subjected to a proper analysis, the gloss rapidly fades. It is interesting that Cardio tennis, with low-compression balls, is promoted in secondary schools – an activity which, by the LTA's own definition, is a 'fitness workout on court', with no technique required. As pointed out in the last chapter, it is probably no good asking the Cardio instructor for any specific technical advice. Considering that secondary school pupils are still at an important development stage technically, Cardio tennis, with all that it implies, is the worst coaching for them to attend.

Mini tennis is also recommended for older beginners because it can offer 'rapid progression' and help change the perception that tennis is too difficult. However, sound coaching is still very much needed at mini tennis level because, when the same youngsters try to play tennis on a normal-size court with normal yellow balls, they will find it very hard to control their shots if they were not taught properly when they were using smaller racquets and softer balls.

It is almost like dumbing the sport down just to get the numbers up.

And how long will these youngsters persist with tennis if they do not learn the basics first?

'Two million children' have presumably been introduced to the sport over the last few years, but how many of them will be inspired to play regularly in their free time, and continue to play regularly when they are adults? I await the figures with bated breath.

When I first realised the predicament that PE teachers were in when it came to teaching tennis, I offered a free half-day course on how to do it properly. About twelve local PE teachers came along, all of whom with experience of LTA courses, or of teaching tennis in their schools. At the end of the half-day I had organised, one of the teachers said that she had just been on an LTA course and that none of what I had shown them that morning had been covered. She added that my instruction was so much better and easier to pass on, and also that it was much more relevant to the sport.

She was even pleased that what she had learnt from me that morning had helped her with her own game as well.

Naturally, all those attending wanted to know why they had not been given much better training on their LTA courses, with one teacher pointing out it had been so bad that she had no intention of using it anyway, and was thinking of going back to a system she had devised herself. How many times have I heard that statement, even from qualified tennis coaches?

However, having been on my half-day course, she was now very happy because it had given her real basics to teach, would get her pupils rallying properly, and also, importantly, enjoying a realistic experience of tennis at the same time.

I do not consider that the instruction I gave these teachers was particularly brilliant – quite the contrary: it was based on common sense and what I had worked out over the years as a grass-roots tennis coach.

I have also, in the past, made arrangements with a primary school for a year six class to visit my tennis academy to receive coaching on actual tennis courts, rather than in an assembly hall, or suchlike. As a 'link', this might be more productive, and more inspiring, in terms of creating interest, than coaches simply going into schools to advertise their clubs, especially since Aegon, as I understand it, are planning not to provide funding for schools tennis from 2014 for financial reasons. Of course, I do appreciate that this ideal introduction to tennis often creates tremendous logistical hurdles for schools to overcome, but, for some, it could perhaps be feasible.

On the 20th June, 2011, an article appeared in 'The Telegraph', stating the following: 'Golf in the UK has left British tennis trailing far behind... Every (golf) club has a teaching professional who helps get players started and to a certain level'.

We are world-beaters at golf and, yet, it would be very difficult to find a school that teaches the sport. A similar situation occurs with cycling and snooker: not taught in schools, but, as a nation, we are outstanding at both.

The conclusion has to be that it is not essential to teach a sport in schools in order to produce world-class players, but, what is absolutely essential, of course, is the quality of the coaching, wherever it takes place.

I know some golf pros who would laugh incredulously at the DVDs produced by the LTA for PE teachers. And, if some teachers on the DVD praise the LTA course, it is simply because they have no experience of tennis or tennis coaching, and are grateful for any ideas about how to proceed, even if some might have reservations about one or two activities. After all, they are being instructed by tennis professionals, so who are they to start questioning things?

We simply have to do it better if we are to get out of the mess we are in: not just tick the box and hopefully increase the numbers playing, but 'get players started' in the right way – i.e. give them sound fundamentals so that they can reach 'a certain level' quickly, no matter what their ability.

It is quite possible to do – I have achieved it many times.

CHAPTER 7

Competitions

Many people are of the opinion that lots of organised competitions are a key factor for success in tennis: the younger you start and the more you compete, the more likely you are to have a chance of making it. Some even claim that giving youngsters the opportunity to compete regularly is the only way to get the cream to rise to the top.

I am sure that the American, Brad Gilbert, brought in a few years ago by the LTA to help British tennis by, among other things, 'upskilling' – their word – our coaches and inspiring the next generation to follow in Andy Murray's footsteps, would be very impressed with the quotation in the last chapter on schools referring to the numbers competing on a tennis court. May I remind you that the quote comes from the 'Written evidence submitted by the LTA and the Tennis Foundation' to the House of Commons Education Committee in March, 2013, and states that 'more than 46,000 pupils took part in a schools tennis competition' in 2012, and, what is more, the same number do this 'each summer'. And these are mostly players who have yet to become really serious about the sport.

I mention the probability of Brad Gilbert being impressed

because, in 2007, a fellow coach and I, quite by chance, found ourselves in the company of the famous man, in charge of coaching Andy Murray at the time, as the three of us were walking towards the Wimbledon Championships, and we had a short conversation with him on this very subject.

When asked why he thought that Great Britain lagged so far behind the rest of the world in tennis, he was most adamant about the reason: 'Not enough competitive play for juniors – they must get out there playing more tournaments and matches. That's where they really learn and improve'. He was absolutely convinced that lack of competition in the earlier years was the one and only reason for our players later failing on the world stage.

While I cannot deny that competing in lots of matches teaches a player to cope with different game styles and to think tactically in order to win, this book essentially points to another, more fundamental, and very British reason for our constant failures over the decades. It is a reason that will become increasingly clear to you, the reader, as you move through the different chapters.

I am honestly not surprised that Brad Gilbert was not aware of this major problem, since, like me, it comes from the very bottom of tennis in the UK – the grass roots, which are a million miles away from the world that he inhabits.

Returning to the subject of competitions, it can be argued that a lack of match play is not necessarily detrimental to a young player's development: there have been many world-ranked players, including household names like Serena and Venus Williams, who were kept away from competitive play throughout most of their junior lives; and there are yet others who, having restricted the number of tournaments they entered in their early years, still come through and achieve success on the professional circuit.

It is highly likely that Brad Gilbert saw our top juniors performing poorly in matches and, therefore, concluded that it was down to a lack of match play experience, and I fully accept that this may well contribute in part to standards that leave a lot to be desired, but it is not the complete answer, in my opinion.

So, let us look at some competitions that are known as 'Grade 7' tournaments. These are for players who are just starting out in tennis. You can even, in theory, begin competing at the age of four! Once again, we are very much at grass-roots level, and, once again, we are in a world that is virtually unknown to people like Brad Gilbert.

It should also be made clear that these competitions are of sufficient importance to count towards a player's rating, which will be very useful later on when the youngster wants to enter higher grade tournaments, and eventually tries to gain national ranking points when he is older.

I wonder how many of you know of the numerous bad experiences a junior has to go through when he first plays in Grade 7 tournaments, because I can assure you that it is enough to deter forever more any aspiring youngster, with or without potential. Once a junior has progressed beyond this early stage of 'starter tournaments' to the higher level Grade 3, 4 and 5 competitions, everything generally seems to run quite well, with the player's mini tennis rating and recent form being fully considered by the county Talent and Performance Coordinator when he decides upon seedings and suitability for entry into the tournament in question.

It has to be said, though, that there are some adverse comments heard from time to time about how highly regulated the structure is for such events, with rules that can unfairly keep a youngster competing at too low a level, when he is obviously ready to take on a more demanding challenge.

Nevertheless, for those wishing to gain their first experience of competitive play, it is not at all good – in fact, it can be, and often is, a real nightmare.

On the LTA website you can 'Find a Competition', where, while the explanation about the tournaments has certainly improved in recent times, along with how it is presented, I still hear of many parents struggling to get their heads around it all.

For your first competitive experience, the website clearly indicates that you should search for a Grade 7 competition. To do so, you are invited to enter the criteria that meet your needs to find the appropriate starter tournament: boys or girls, age group, area, etc., having already stipulated 'Grade 7', which the website readily accepts.

But, having entered the information, you will be disappointed to discover that there are no tournaments which match your criteria. If you wait a few months, or widen the area in which you are prepared to travel, you will still be informed that there are no tournaments for you. The truth is, Grade 7 tournaments are not listed on the website. It is very much a case of 'Computer says, No', to quote from a *Little Britain* sketch.

Why then do the LTA not provide this highly useful information from the outset? Why invite the novice tournament player, and his parents, possibly visiting the LTA website for the first time, to search for Grade 7 competitions when they do not appear to exist, and why not flag this up with an explanation when someone types in 'Grade 7' as part of their search? The only indication on the website that something is different about the Grade 7s is that they are in-house, but nothing to make it clear that they are rarely advertised on the LTA website. The reason being that it is up to individual clubs to organise such tournaments internally.

Even though I have pointed this problem out to my county organiser, my concerns have always fallen on deaf ears. The question has to be asked: how are parents ever going to find an 'internal tournament' for their offspring if they are not listed on the LTA website, especially if they do not happen to be pursuing their tennis at a club, or they are at a club which does not offer Grade 7 tournaments, for whatever reason, possibly because it does not have a viable number of youngsters, or the coach is not energetic enough to organise things, etc.?

In my own area I know of several people who have volunteered to act as tournament referees, but have had to cancel Grade 7 competitions because of lack of interest, even after making them open to outsiders. Then I hear requests for more junior starter tournaments from parents.

I often receive a desperate telephone call from such referees asking if I can send some juniors along to boost the numbers. Sometimes I can, but other times the notice has come too late for me to help, and I subsequently hear that the tournament has been cancelled due to insufficient entries. The impact of this one problem alone is huge, when keen and often talented juniors, excited at the prospect of their first tournament, are let down, and volunteers attempting to stage such a tournament, with all the hard work it entails, have wasted their valuable time.

What a ridiculous situation for British tennis to be in with regard to introducing juniors to their first competitive tournament.

And when I have turned up to watch Grade 7 tournaments, usually because some of my pupils are playing, too often the event is so poorly organised that it is enough to put any sporty youngster off. The referee may be welcoming, and may well try to run things to the best of his ability, but, sadly, all too often he falls short of the standards one would expect.

Here is a list of what frequently happens:

- A round robin group producing a winner based on total number of games won, not matches won, is suddenly foreshortened due to time constraints, causing a strong player not to qualify because he has played fewer games than his opponents;
- The semi-final of the main event is put on the only poorly-surfaced court with a net that is too low and cannot be adjusted, while, at the same time, a first round of the consolation event is put on the best court;
- Juniors are asked to umpire matches, but they are far too young to be expected to do the job properly, giving rise to as many as two incorrect decisions in every game;
- The referee umpires the final, but is so interrupted by players and friends saying their goodbyes that he continually returns to the match with the wrong score, declaring the winners as losers. The players are only six years of age and it all ends in tears;
- In one tournament with an entry of fourteen boys, they are all placed into one round robin group, with not a hope of thirteen matches, however short, ever being played by any one competitor, and the declared winner on this occasion is the boy who happens to be undefeated, having played four of the weakest entrants;
- A straightforward knockout event ends up with three players reaching the final, turning it into a huge anti-climax, because the volunteer referee of thirty years' experience

cannot organise the draw so that only two meet in the said final, the reason being that he has never heard of a 'bye';

- Having had the 'bye' explained to him, he makes the same mistake the following year, this time inserting a bye for one of the two semi-finals;

- The referee, only using first names to call players for matches, twice puts the wrong 'James' on court because, confusingly for him, another entrant is also called James;

- In a red ball tournament the referee mistakenly faults a six year-old for volleying, and immediately announces to all competitors that volleying is not permitted.

My co-author advises me to stop here, but I do have many more examples of the unholy mess caused by these refereeing nightmares, and I would like to carry on a little longer and give some more instances of the disappointments that juniors have to put up with, in this case when playing team tennis at grass-roots level. My co-author has reacted by saying it is just what he expected of me – I wonder if that is a compliment?

When it comes to inter-club, junior league tennis, the frequent chaos that prevails is quite unbelievable – so much so, that, during the time I ran my academy, I refused to enter a junior team in the league because there were more cancellations than matches being played. One local league collapsed because too many fixtures were simply never completed.

When I used to coach my junior squads at one of the participating clubs on Saturday mornings, on several occasions I witnessed visiting junior teams arriving to find that there were no opponents. Once, the embarrassed organiser hurried over to where I was coaching and poached four of my squad players so that they could provide some sort of opposition for the visitors.

Only a few years ago I asked two coaches at other bases whether they entered teams in the junior league. One replied it was a waste of time, owing to the unreliability of other teams, and the other informed me that he did, but that he always arranged for four extra juniors to turn up for home matches so that they could all mix in and stage a team match among themselves when the opposition failed to arrive.

What a sad state of affairs. But this is the reality of junior competitive tennis at grass-roots level in Britain, at least in my neck of the woods. These are the facts – I have not made them up. To say that such a mess is unfair on our juniors is an understatement.

I am sure that such incompetence at grass-roots level would shock Brad Gilbert, especially as he considers competitive play for juniors to be so crucial. It should also have already shocked and galvanised the LTA, but, as we have already seen, reality of this kind does not form part of their world.

It is indeed ironic that the LTA have been putting so much emphasis on increasing participation in tennis, a real 'all hands to the pump' job, and yet keen juniors, and their parents, are being constantly turned off the sport in this way. And remember, the examples I have given are by no means isolated ones – I have lots more that it has been my misfortune to come across all too often, but I will listen to my co-author on this occasion, and spare you any further examples of the kind of disorganisation that exists at Grade 7 tournament level.

When I inform my county Tennis Association of the serious problems with these tournaments, they show polite concern, but do nothing to rectify them. Since the salaried tennis county personnel do not attend the said tournaments, they are oblivious to the problems of juniors and parents who are not informed properly about these events, do not know about tournaments being cancelled, and do not witness for themselves the frequent, shambolic refereeing when they do actually take place. At least, they are in good company – the LTA are equally ignorant of what goes on.

The message I am given by the county is loud and clear: they have always done it this way; it is not LTA policy to advertise Grade 7 tournaments on the LTA website; it is up to the referees to invite juniors from other local tennis bases to take part if they need more players; and there are LTA courses that teach people how to referee tournaments, should anyone need guidance.

So the powers that be simply do not consider that there is a problem – everything is in place to enable it all to run smoothly. Unfortunately, quite the opposite is true, and, if those working in tennis could come down to my humble level – a difficult journey for them, I know – they would very quickly see what I am complaining about, and might even muster up enough energy to change the system. I have made some concrete suggestions as to how to improve things, especially as to how to ensure new juniors to the game are notified of Grade 7 tournaments, but all to no avail.

It is also a sad fact that the majority of those who take on the job of running these tournaments have never attended a referees' course because they do not even know of their existence, and, anyway, one does sometimes have to question quite seriously the suitability of those who volunteer for such tasks in the first place.

Often, a referee will report that the tournament he has run has been a success, but the truth is, he is blithely unaware of the poor decisions he has made, or just chooses to forget about them. The tournament staggers falteringly to an unimpressive finish, with the winner and his family possibly the only people to derive any satisfaction from the experience.

More than once, I have heard parents say quite categorically that their child would never play in a particular tournament again, not because of sour grapes, but because of the chaos they had witnessed. They have even handed me copies of letters of complaint, thinking and wishing that I could do something about a tournament they had been to elsewhere. There is a solution to all this, which I have spoken up about to my county association, but inertia is the order of the day.

How is this fun? (a word that is so dear to the LTA). How does this encourage players new to competitive tennis to continue? For juniors, especially younger juniors, and those playing in a tournament for the first time, it is their Wimbledon: it is, or should be, the highlight of their time in tennis so far; and, for players with more serious intentions, it is a terrible introduction to tournament play.

As a junior myself, having played in hundreds of table tennis and tennis tournaments over thirty years ago, I never experienced anything like the shambles that I have seen far too often at this lower end of junior tennis. And I must emphasise that the examples I have given are definitely not rare occurrences, otherwise I would not have gone to the trouble of writing this chapter.

Once again, it is the reality of what is happening at grass-roots level. The sad thing is, of course, that sporty children, how many, we shall never know, will have already left tennis for better-organised sports at which they also are starting to excel. And it is a trend that will continue unless the appallingly amateurish nature of starter tournaments is put right.

While it is true that the main thrust of this book is to point to a reason other than that of competitions for the constant failures of British tennis to produce world-class players, it has to be recognised that what is described in this chapter does not help the situation one iota.

How can we afford to lose youngsters in this way by allowing such a mess to continue? And should the LTA not be more professional in the way they promote and stage their tennis events at this level? After all, they pride themselves in leading the way for sport generally on so many other fronts.

Someone, anyone!, please take note. And, hopefully, do something.

CHAPTER 8

Commentators and Presenters

My co-author remembers two very well-known BBC TV sports presenters predicting, some twenty-five years ago, that tennis was about to take off in Great Britain because of the advent of satellite television, meaning that the sport was going to be shown live on our screens all the year round, and not just during the Wimbledon fortnight. We Brits would be inspired to go out and play the game in our droves, participation figures would rocket, and, from all the younger cohorts, champions would emerge. Tennis in this country was on the verge of being transformed, they said. We all know only too well that it did not happen – it was yet another false dawn.

It is my view that the great increase in the televising of tennis in the UK over the last two decades has, ironically, contributed to the mess we are in and the problems we have in producing top 100 players. This is the theme of the present chapter.

There is no doubt whatsoever, in my opinion, that commentators and presenters do a very good job in setting the scene for each tournament, and in preparing the viewers for upcoming matches. They conduct interviews with the players, provide information on rankings, past achievements, and different styles of play; they analyse the matches afterwards and talk about the tactics employed, etc. In short, they create interest for all viewers, whether they are active tennis players, or just armchair ones.

However, tennis, like football and golf, is a sport with a high percentage of junior viewers who actually play the game as well. Youngsters will try out tactical tips given by football pundits, like Gary Neville, who analyse the moves of their heroes after a match; during golf tournaments, Denis Pugh is one of several experts giving excellent tips on the technique used by leading players, and the power of television is such that millions of viewers will be influenced by any comments made on how to play, and will most likely go and try the advice out for themselves the next day.

This is how it is, and how it should be, and young players not only enjoy learning about their sport in this way, but for most, it is the only coaching they receive, and virtually the only opportunity they have of improving. Indeed, it was my way of trying to improve, watching Wimbledon players and doing my best with the commentators' tips on anything and everything. But somehow, despite the great contribution tennis commentators make to our enjoyment and appreciation of the sport, they fail quite spectacularly on any technical advice they offer, as you are about to see.

A real live tennis coach costs money, so advice from TV should be the next best thing, but it is not. The influence of television is enormous, of course – it reaches out to millions. If I teach a topspin forehand drive to a group of eight juniors, I only influence those eight juniors, and nobody else, and, what is more, they can question me in order to get things really clear in their minds.

But they cannot question the person talking on TV, so they have to take it all at face value, interpret it as best they can, and go and practise it the next time they play. And, if 3 million viewers have just heard advice that is wrong or misleading, they are not going to improve, and, sadly, they may now be worse players than they were before the commentator's remarks.

During commentary on a match it is common to hear phrases like: 'Great backhand – and all done with a flick of the wrist'.

The keen tennis player, wanting to get better, will try this on court. I know, as a coach, that it will not work, and, incidentally, if the backhand in question were shown in slow motion, it would be clearly seen that the wrist was NOT flicked. And sometimes the shot IS shown in slow motion, and still no one points it out. We also hear: 'He rolls the racquet over the ball for topspin'. In reality, rolling the wrist actually prevents topspin and creates something called unforced errors.

I remember one occasion, when Venus Williams was playing, she had lost the first set because of the many mistakes she was making with her forehand drive. The commentator said, by way of explanation: 'She will never get her forehand in with a bent arm like that'. In the second set Venus turned the match around completely, hitting winner after winner from her forehand side, still with the forbidden bent arm, but no further comment was heard on the matter.

Sure enough, the following week I had to correct a customer who, having picked up on what the commentator had said, was now trying to hit his forehand drive with a rigid and straight arm, and was unsurprisingly making a real hash of the shot. Before the comment on TV his forehand drive had been going well, and it was only because of my intervention that he was able to resurrect his old and successful way of hitting it. But what about the millions with no input other than what they had heard on TV?

Players following the examples I have given so far of technically incorrect comments will have tried to improve their game by hitting forehand drives with a straight and rigid arm, impart topspin by rolling their wrists, and flick the same part of their anatomy for all their backhands. With no one to tell them differently, they have quite frankly no chance of learning how to play properly: in technical terms, the faults they will develop in their drives could not be more serious. Is it any wonder that bad habits are developed by our juniors, and older players too?

By no means am I exaggerating when I make these statements: because my approach to coaching is very different from that of most other coaches, I have been able to clear players' minds many times of such damaging advice before they have been in a position to make any real progress. And, of course, if bad habits have become ingrained, it is not easy to get the player back on the right path again.

Commentating is one thing, coaching is another, and the two most certainly do not go together on British television. And, even if a commentator is an ex-professional tennis player, he is still not a coach.

John McEnroe once stood up to demonstrate to the assembled press the way he played his forehand volley, so brilliant had it been in beating Ivan Lendl in a big final: what he showed them with his racquet was completely different from what he had actually done on court, although he thought it was one and the same thing. The reason for this is that a high-level player executes his shots instinctively like an automaton, without thinking and without analysing – in effect, he does not know what he is doing, he just does it; a coach, on the other hand, constantly analyses in order to break the strokes of the game down so that his pupils can learn properly, one step at a time.

In my own case, it was only when I became a coach that I actually discovered for the first time what I did well as a player and, incidentally, what I also did rather badly too. Before that, I just played my matches, thinking only tactically, and not technically.

And so it goes on.

The German player, Angelique Kerber who is top 10 at the time of writing, was described as 'really wrapping her wrist around the ball' to get extra topspin, by a commentator, British, of course, who had played for several years on the professional circuit. Not only is this remark very misleading – it could also easily lead to an injury.

The talented Latvian, Ernests Gulbis, usually in the top 50 and always a threat to the elite, was referred to by another British ex-professional player, turned commentator, as having a very 'unorthodox' forehand drive. I can assure you, and him, that his technique is like that of any other top player, otherwise the ball would not go in the court when hit so hard, sometimes, in the Latvian's case, at over 100 mph.

The fact is that top players all hit their shots so well by remaining technically within certain parameters. The slight, or at times seemingly big, difference between their various strokes is called their style, but their technique is actually the same.

The only thing that makes Gulbis's forehand drive look different is his very early take-back of the racquet. Again, there is little understanding shown by the commentator of the nuts and bolts of a tennis stroke.

Another former top British player analysed a backhand drive passing shot played by Greg Rusedski at Wimbledon one year. The replay was paused in the backswing position, just before contact with the ball. I waited for enlightening comments about any one of the five technical fundamentals which ALL top players display at this point when playing this stroke.

Remarkably, with the still frame showing clearly all five fundamentals, our former top player failed to refer to even one of them. Instead, all he could offer was: 'Look how closely Greg keeps his eyes on the ball, and all you have to do from here is fling your racquet through'.

From the technically perfect backswing position on view, Greg could possibly have just swung his racquet through, but the technique which he actually employed was superb – the result, as one would expect, of honing the shot during hours and hours of practice.

A novice, on the other hand, whether at grass-roots level or just above, would not have a hope of doing so without the right guidance. In what way does the instruction 'just fling the racquet through' tell anyone about how to hit the shot?

My golf professional tells me that, if he made a similar remark to a customer learning how to play golf, he would expect them to walk away in disgust and never return.

The only other piece of advice given by the former player turned commentator was basically 'watch the ball', which is totally unnecessary because absolutely everybody watches the ball on a tennis court, even when playing for the very first time, otherwise there would be no attempted swing of the racquet at the ball.

I do, however, have to report, sadly, that the completely inane 'just fling the racquet through' is not too far away from the equally inane 'Load and explode', heard on a recent LTA training course for coaches. And 'Watch the ball', by the way, has been a catchphrase used for years in this country in order to explain why someone mishits, or even completely misses, the ball, when, as you will read in a later chapter, taking your eyes off the ball is not the reason for mishits. I have yet to see the instruction to 'watch the ball' actually work on a tennis court.

Here is yet another example – there have been so many over the years: Andy Roddick had just broken the world record for the fastest serve at the Queen's Club. Sue Barker asked her British colleague the very reasonable and interesting question: 'Where does Andy get his power from?'.

Thousands upon thousands of ears, belonging to junior, and not so junior, tennis players all over the country, must have pricked up in eager anticipation of the answer, which was: 'Just listen to the thwack as his racquet hits the ball'. The BBC then replayed Roddick's serve five times and repeated this gem of a comment on each occasion. In case you do not know, there are at least four factors which contribute to power on the serve, but, obviously, the analyst, an ex-player, thought differently – 'just listen to the thwack' and you too can have a serve like Roddick's.

As I suggested at the beginning of Chapter 5, if we were German, we would simply not stand for it. Indeed, I am confident that, if it were the sport of golf which was being covered, even we in Britain would protest for a change and not put up with such meaningless remarks.

Why do we have to be so amateurish and undemanding when it comes to tennis? Why does no one from the LTA Coaching Department come forward and put it right? Can you imagine a golf commentator asking us just 'to listen to the ping' to explain where Tiger Woods gets his power from when driving a ball more than 300 yards? There would be howls of protest from viewers and golf professionals alike, and we would probably never see or hear the commentator again.

And it does not get any better with the passing of time: the Canadian Milos Raonic, semifinalist at Wimbledon in 2014, had his 140mph service analysed on TV, and the conclusion reached was that his racquet position and grip at the start of his action were most peculiar, with the grip being described as 'weak'. The inference to our juniors, and anyone else, for that matter, was not to copy the Wimbledon semifinalist and top 10 player. How ridiculous! As a technically aware coach, I have been teaching players for some time to adopt Raonic's set-up position for the serve, and to hold the racquet with the strong - not 'weak' - grip that he uses, precisely because what Raonic does produces a faster delivery. Oh, what a sorry mess we are in when such wonderful opportunities to educate the public are wasted.

And if you can stand it, a few years ago, incredible as it may seem, there was even a tennis commentator who had no idea of the difference between topspin, flat and slice, and would sometimes marvel at what he thought was a 'topspin' forehand winner hit by Pete Sampras, although, it must be said, he usually referred just to 'backhands' and 'forehands' with no epithet added. On one occasion, his fellow commentator, who was both a coach and high-level player, had to correct the misleading description by saying: 'That was not topspin – Sampras hit it as flat as a pancake'. However, the same commentator was allowed to continue in his job for years – no one from on high deemed it necessary to take any action at all.

In terms of technical knowledge, tennis presenters and commentators, although not as bad as the one just described, are light years away from those of other sports on British television. The language they use is so imprecise and woolly, whereas it could, and should, be a hundred times better. There are constant references to 'forehands' and 'backhands', but quite often nothing is said about the type of forehand or backhand that has been played. If we were listening to a radio commentary, the sport being described could easily be squash, or badminton, or table tennis, since all three have forehands and backhands. It would be so much more instructive if the backhand, for example, could have 'topspin', 'slice' or 'half-volley' added to it. So much more could be done to educate the general public, including juniors, of course, and to give them a greater understanding of the sport.

It is not surprising that, when I ask a class of eight adult beginners to name some tennis strokes, all I get by way of reply is: 'forehand, backhand, and serve'; and then, occasionally, someone manages to remember another: 'the volley'. Most beginners truly believe that there are only three or four shots in tennis, whereas, in fact, there are more than twenty.

And the idea that a professional has a choice of spin every time the ball comes over the net has never entered their heads, and I can apply that remark to many club players with years of experience, as well as beginners. They have learnt this from television, of course.

In contrast, if I ask the same question of beginners in a table tennis class, they are so much more knowledgeable, and come up with 'forehand push', 'backhand counter hit', 'forehand loop', 'topspin', 'chop', etc.

I am of the opinion that tennis is the only sport on British television and radio that suffers in this way: in cricket, accurate technical terms are used to describe what happens on the field of play, and there is frequent and detailed analysis of how the professionals on show succeed, or fail, in what they are doing; in snooker, commentators use expressions like 'excellent stun shot', 'played with a terrific amount of left-hand side', or 'great screw back', all accompanied by an explanation of the term if necessary. You would never hear: 'That was a great hit on the cue ball'; similarly, in ice-skating, the commentator never says: 'That was a great jump', but, rather: 'That was a great double Salchow' or 'triple Lutz'.

The irony is that most viewers, in practical terms, do not need to know which type of jump has just been performed because they are highly unlikely ever to attempt such a thing, unless they want to end up on crutches, of course. However, many viewers, being tennis players, occasional or otherwise, would love to try hitting the ball with topspin, for example, so any proper technical advice on this would be well received, but it is simply not forthcoming.

So many opportunities have been lost over the years to show the public just how sophisticated and varied the sport of tennis is. Through constantly poor technical commentating many viewers never appreciated that the great Steffi Graf only ever played a backhand slice in her matches, while her opponents would nearly always play backhand drives when trading shots with her cross court.

So much could have been explained on this one aspect alone, so much extra interest could have been created, not least among keen grass-roots players, but, as it was, for most viewers Steffi Graf vs A. N. Other was just another tennis match with the ball going backwards and forwards over the net – in truth, all rather boring.

There was once a relatively unknown player, whose name unfortunately escapes me, taking part in a televised match in the Queen's Club tournament that is held just prior to Wimbledon. He had double-handed drives on both sides, but, unusually, he swapped his hands over on the grip of his racquet so that he always played a backhand, and therefore never a forehand. What happened was that, on his left-hand side, he hit the ball with topspin with a right-handed, double-handed backhand drive, and, on his right-hand side, because he swapped his hands over, he hit the ball, also with topspin, with a left-handed, double-handed backhand drive.

The bemused commentator was ecstatic about what he was witnessing – 'Have you ever seen a forehand played like that before?' – but it was quite beyond him to work out what was really happening: i.e. that the player was ambidextrous and did not actually possess a forehand drive!

And a full hour later, he was still highlighting the strange forehand to the viewers, so, not only had he not become aware of the two double-handed backhand drives he was commentating on, but it was obvious that all his colleagues in the studio were none the wiser either, and were unable to put him right.

Can you imagine a commentator on snooker not realising that Ronnie O'Sullivan often does not need to use the rest because he is also ambidextrous, and plays shots left-handed as well as right-handed?

During the 2013 US Open a top lady player had been struggling with her ball toss when serving. The presenters in the studio, all former high-ranking players, started discussing how one should throw the ball up to serve. They all had different ideas on how to hold the ball, and how one should throw it into the air, and actually fumbled around with a ball for some time, trying out various options.

In my own experience of tennis, I can say honestly that, as a county player, I had no idea of how I threw the ball up, and yet I never had a problem with this part of my game, presumably because I did it the right way. Later, as a coach, I discovered that I did do it correctly, and, after picking the brains of top coaches from around the world during a trip to the USA, I learnt that there is actually only one way to hold the ball, and two ways to throw it up for serving.

As it happens, over 95% of players, no matter what level they are at, do the correct thing quite naturally. Unfortunately, the remaining 5% who did need help that day would have still been in a mess if they had followed the tips they had heard on TV.

When it comes to tennis, the whole mindset of those who work for TV and radio is wrong. During the 2013 US Open the presenter on Sky Sports asked about the technique for the topspin backhand drive. Sitting beside him were Greg Rusedski and Judy Murray, one an ex-player and the other a coach. It should have been logical for him at least to ask the coach at some stage, but he did not – he only asked Greg Rusedski, who, with racquet in hand, showed the shape of the stroke. That was it – all over in a few seconds, when he could easily have had longer, and immediately the conversation turned to something else.

From a teaching point of view, it could have been so much more instructive if the nuts and bolts of the shot – grip, preparation, angle of racquet, contact point, follow-through, etc. – had been explained by the coach, Judy Murray, but she was not even invited to make a contribution. Of course, if you are an ex-top 10 player, it is assumed by the media – quite erroneously – that you are the best person to ask about technique, whereas, in reality, it is the coach who understands how it all works, and is the best person to explain it and teach it.

And this is why they always get it right during the TV coverage of golf: former top stars of the game comment on the tournament play, but when it comes to analysing the swing in the studio, the responsibility is passed over to a coach like Denis Pugh or Scott Cranfield, who always give accurate and precise analysis of shots. You would never see them looking bewildered and wondering how to address the ball, or swing at it.

During the 2013 French Open, one of the commentators, who was also an ex-player, was shown on television trying to teach an absolute beginner how to impart topspin on the ball like the professionals. The tennis enthusiast – a lady – insisted on top-spinning with a single-handed backhand, but, still holding the racquet with a forehand grip, she was asked to use her wrist more after a couple of hopeless attempts.

Without improving at all her chances of executing the shot correctly, the advice to use her wrist more was increasing the possibility of injury. I know I have said this before, but it is important, especially if you are the one who ends up injured.

What I find interesting, though, is how the commentator and the beginner left the court together in giggles, both accepting, and giving the impression to millions of viewers, that it was the lady's fault she had failed so miserably, when the truth is, it was the commentator who had failed miserably with his coaching.

A good coach would get such a person on the right lines straightaway because that is his job. How off-putting must the sight of the commentator and lady beginner have been for viewers, young and not so young, who were thinking of giving tennis a go.

On a slightly different tack now. As human beings we are all seduced by fame: if you are a well-known, British, ex-professional player and commentator, and are asked about how much it costs a year to try and make it in tennis, whatever you say carries weight and is believed, even if you are guessing. And, if the sum of money quoted is an enormous one, the reaction of parents with sporty offspring who are keen on tennis can easily be imagined: 'Right, that's it. You're only playing football from now on'.

Such a comment, in all its misleading glory, was made in July, 2013, during a radio discussion about the Andy Murray effect the day after he had won Wimbledon.

The former professional player and commentator in question had quoted a sum of £25,000 to £35,000 a year for a junior to have any chance of following in the footsteps of Andy Murray.

Was he really not aware of the detrimental effect his words would have had on parents thinking of enrolling their offspring on a coaching course? With the summer holidays fast approaching, the comment could not have been more badly timed.

But, of more importance, every tennis coach I know would quote nothing like this sum. For your information, any junior who attended my academy would have had all the tennis and coaching required for around £2,000 a year, and less in their earlier years. And this is without any LTA funding, sponsorship deals, or money from the Wimbledon profits, which could be used for really promising juniors.

One person who is asked about tennis and the technique of the sport when he is in this country is Nick Bollettieri, and what a treat it is to hear his explanations of how to play the strokes of the game. He is always precise, clear and to the point, in complete contrast to what we normally get in Great Britain. But, then, he is a coach, and, just as important for the media, of course, he is very famous, so he is definitely a person to have as part of the commentary team.

It is interesting that Mr. Bollettieri '...never played competitive tennis' (page ix of *My Aces, My Faults*, by Nick Bollettieri and Dick Schaap) and yet, his opinions and thoughts on the sport and the technique required to play it are constantly sought after and valued.

What a muddle and a mess it all is here. Not only are wonderful opportunities missed, but the advice, when given, is often misleading and unhelpful, to say the least.

In contrast, for people wanting to learn to play golf, there are good coaching programmes on TV, as well as many five-minute slots during tournaments every week with tips on technique; for tennis there is virtually nothing.

There was, however, an effort made once by Channel 4 to provide something in the nature of tennis coaching, but it was far from inspiring, or even instructive. It went out as a coaching tip at the end of each transmission of a tournament, and lasted only a few minutes.

It was fronted by an ex-professional British player, and I waited with bated breath to hear what he had to say. Unfortunately, the whole tone of the slot was frivolous in the extreme, and nothing of note was said to help the viewer with his tennis.

At the end of each programme the former world-ranked player came out with a tongue-in-cheek comment: 'Don't forget your racquet because you cannot play without it'; next time his coaching tip was: 'Don't forget to take some balls or you won't be able to have a game'.

Despite complaints to Channel 4, pointing out that they were wasting a great opportunity to help juniors and adults wanting to improve, and that they were also causing embarrassment for the sport of tennis, their response was: 'We take tennis far too seriously in this country which is not an encouragement for youngsters to get involved', and they 'saw no problem with having a bit of humour in a tennis programme'.

No wonder Sue Barker exclaimed at the end of a day's Wimbledon coverage, when Tim Henman first made an impact: 'At last British tennis is no longer a joke!'

I suppose that we could once again say the same thing, now that Andy Murray has won Wimbledon, but, with 'fun' being so dominant in our teaching of the sport, I do tend to think that the Channel 4 attitude is still very much alive and well.

And, remember, Andy Murray has taken tennis very seriously since about the age of three, so I have heard, and as far as I can work out.

In short, there has been nothing of substance for decades on our TV screens that teaches people how to get the ball over the net with the basic techniques necessary for the main strokes of the game.

How can anyone get to learn to play tennis in this country?

With the Channel 4 efforts on giving tips on tennis in mind, it is very relevant here to ask the following: would we ever hear comments like 'Don't forget to bring your clubs and some balls next time' in a TV programme on how to play golf?

As has been seen in previous chapters, and will also be very evident later on, there are so many things in Great Britain that are wrong at grass-roots level and above if you want to learn how to play tennis properly, and the mess we are in is most definitely not helped by presenters and commentators on television and radio.

My co-author tells me that commentators on Spanish TV are much better at giving technical advice when the occasion arises: jokes may be indulged in during normal commentary, but, when it comes to tips on technique, the tone is decidedly serious. It is perhaps no coincidence that Spain has the largest pool of professional tennis players in the world, with a good number in the top 100. Of course, this is not just down to advice given on TV – far from it – but it is all part of the jigsaw.

As I wrote at the beginning of the chapter, our commentators and presenters do an excellent job, striking an impressive balance between being informative and entertaining – we simply could not do without them.

However, with regard to that crucial side of tennis called technique, they leave so much to be desired.

And I make no apologies for being so serious and so critical: the mess we are in has been around for far too long for frivolity to be the order of the day.

CHAPTER 9

Being a Coach

It is almost self-evident to say that the coach has an absolutely vital role to play in every sport.

'I had a great coach' was the usual reply of British medal winners at the 2012 Olympics when asked about how they achieved their successes; Sir Alex Ferguson kept Manchester United at the top of football for many, many years, even when pundits said that his squad was not strong enough; Nick Faldo went from being a good professional golfer to being an all-time great by following the technical advice of one coach – David Leadbetter, who changed his technique completely, developing a swing which others on the tour could not live with.

Of course, any successful sportsman or woman has to put in a lot of hard work, be very determined, and make considerable sacrifices, but following the right path is absolutely key. If you have the desire and you work hard on the wrong things, you will get nowhere, but if you have the desire and you work hard on the right things, you will definitely have a chance.

The old saying 'Practice makes perfect' is wrong – a good coach knows that only too well, and will be able to correct it to 'Perfect practice makes perfect'. Without correct guidance in sport you are simply flawed, and virtually doomed to failure.

It is, however, true that very occasionally great sportsmen emerge who do it their own way without purposely following any set procedure, but these are the rarest of exceptions who happen in any case to go down the right path, not because of a coach, but because of their innate genius and the instinctive feeling they have for their particular sport. And if they are honest, in hindsight, they will often admit that they were a little bit lucky in the way they made it. But for the overwhelming majority of those who reach a world-class standard – easily over 90%, in my opinion – the coach and coaching are everything.

We are now approaching the heart of the mess that exists in British tennis. Being a coach is a wonderful occupation: if you are good, you can work miracles, starting at grass-roots level; if you are not good, you can do the opposite, and then, of course, it is not so wonderful. In effect, you hold the trump card for that magic goal in tennis – the top 100!

It does go without saying, however, that I am fully aware parental support is very much an important factor in the success or otherwise of a junior, and, indeed, there are other factors that can come into play as well, but you will see in the next two chapters just how overwhelmingly crucial 'The Coach' and 'Coaching' are for an explanation of the mess we are in, and have been for decades. They point to a reality that seems to have escaped most people. They also – happily – point to a solution.

CHAPTER 10

The Coach

IMPORTANT NOTE ABOUT THE NEXT TWO CHAPTERS: the many examples given of what really goes on in British tennis are mostly based on my own experiences and observations in over twenty-five years of coaching, and those that are not have been thoroughly checked and verified before including them. In short, I have made nothing up – to the best of my knowledge it is all true.

ANOTHER IMPORTANT NOTE, UNUSUAL BUT NECESSARY, put in on the advice of my co-author, who knows much more than I do about books and literary style.

Since this chapter is very long, with many detailed examples, all true, but too many for my co-author, there now follows a summary of the same for the convenience of the reader.

SUMMARY

Coaches are badly treated almost everywhere they teach, and face so many obstacles when they should be focusing on their programmes and developing promising juniors. There is nobody to turn to for support despite paying to be a member of three entities – a coaching organisation, British Tennis and the BTCA, a union for coaches.

No sensible, level-headed person would consider a career as a tennis coach with such a set-up. But, having started out, coaches soon discover the horrors and politics of it all, often ending up quitting, and moving on to another profession. The result is that British tennis loses many potentially good coaches.

Some do not quit, but go abroad – I came across twelve such coaches, as you will see, who left our shores because of all the hassle they had encountered here, and settled in Spain, a country that does produce top players.

HEALTH WARNING!

Please do not try to read this chapter all at once – you may well end up needing anti-depressants and medication for raised blood pressure and giddiness. It is probably best to dip in and out at your pleasure, if that is the right word. It might even be a good idea to come back on different days in order to appreciate more fully the situation of a practising full-time coach.

You will, no doubt, get the gist quite quickly, but some examples – inevitably occurring later on in the chapter – are of a truly horrendous nature, so stick with it, if you can – I am assuming you like a bit of horror. With my co-author's help I have tried to lighten it all up wherever possible so that you, the reader, are not too weighed down and can, at least, find something pleasurable from the wonderful pastime that is reading.

First of all, the coach whose situation I am describing in this chapter is someone who has chosen to teach tennis as a career and is very much full-time.

There are, as you may know, other kinds of coaches who are not full-time – in fact, far from it, because they have another occupation they pursue for five days a week, or more. They therefore view coaching as a useful source of extra income, but by no means do they have the time to be as professional, or committed, as the full-timer. For such people coaching is virtually a hobby, and certainly not a career. They are what I call 'hobby coaches', and this is how I refer to them, both in this chapter and elsewhere.

Coming back now to the full-timer: coaching tennis is his career and therefore very much his livelihood; he is very likely to have a family to support, to be self-employed and to have to fend for himself. As a professional, he needs to be very committed and dedicated to his job. He also needs customers and a base with tennis courts in order to function and, importantly, earn a decent wage.

Those of you who live in the more normal world probably think that having a tennis base and enough customers for the next month would be enough, but, perhaps surprisingly, it is not – equally important is security. It is of no use to any tennis coach, having spent considerable time and effort in building up a coaching business, only to have it suddenly taken away from him, and yet, sadly, this can and does happen more often than you might think. You will be fully apprised of this later on in the chapter.

To give you some idea of just how difficult it is to survive, I would like to compare the profession of a tennis coach with that of a schoolteacher. Not an unreasonable comparison since the tennis coach is only a teacher of tennis, as a schoolteacher is a teacher of geography, for example.

A schoolteacher equally needs customers – his pupils – and a base where he can teach, usually a classroom at a school. Without these two essentials he would not be able to function, just like the tennis coach, and presumably would not be paid. But imagine if there were a constant doubt about retaining the classroom or pupils. Any sensible teacher would surely claim he could not operate under such conditions, and would seriously consider leaving teaching for another profession. So the schoolteacher needs security too, or, at least, a certain degree of security, otherwise, taking up teaching is quite simply a non-starter, and we would not have nearly enough teachers in our schools.

Our schoolteacher and tennis coach are in a very similar position, therefore – both needing somewhere to work and people to teach, with the absolutely essential proviso that the place and the people or pupils, will always be there, so that a decent wage can be earned and be guaranteed.

So let us take our comparison a bit further and assume our tennis coach and schoolteacher have just been offered a job. The schoolteacher starts week one at a school, in a classroom, on full pay from the first day, with no expenses, almost certainly in a pension scheme, and no weather worries, and is guaranteed to have customers while he remains there. Any expenses for equipment to help him with his teaching will be paid for by the school, and he will have to do something drastically wrong for his job to be taken away from him. He probably gets coffee and free lunches thrown in for good measure as well.

The tennis coach, on the other hand, starts week one at a sports centre or tennis club, but does he get paid that week? No, because he has to build up his customer base first. Does he have expenses? Yes, he certainly does: expenses for petrol, administration, advertising, mobile phone calls, court hire, tennis equipment, coaching membership, training courses, etc.

Slowly, week by week, the tennis coach builds up his clientele, and, by the second year, may have a fairly comprehensive programme, earning an average wage or better, if he is lucky, but probably still with debts from year one's lowly income.

And the tennis coach will certainly have worked longer hours too, with no pension or sick pay, and often experiencing lost revenue because of inclement weather and customers not turning up from time to time.

In contrast, the schoolteacher can lose half his class for various reasons, such as sickness, school trips or exams, but he still receives his full salary. What an outcry there would be, if each week a teacher's pay packet were reduced according to the number of pupils missing from each lesson. And it is not as though the teacher has ever had to find any pupils for himself in the first place either.

I must make clear here that it is not my intention to be the grumpy old man of tennis coaching: I am well aware that the coach is self-employed, and the above facts are part and parcel of most self-employed professions. But, nevertheless, these considerations of less pay, with longer working hours and unavoidable extra expenses in the first few months, are serious concerns which a coach has to take into account before deciding on coaching as a career and accepting a job on a self-employed basis, which is what the vast majority of coaching positions entail.

The truth is, then, that I am not being grumpy at all because I am well aware of this disparity between tennis coaches and schoolteachers, especially in the first year of the job, and fully accept the extra difficulties encountered early on, but **only** on the understanding that the tennis coach can benefit fully from his hard work from year two, and beyond.

It is no good being a tennis coach if there is considerable doubt about surviving the first year with all the work and settling in required. But this is where the problem lies and what this chapter is all about.

Years two and three, and beyond, have to be a reality for the tennis coach, but too often, despite working very hard and earnestly, and keeping to the letter of the agreed conditions, the coach's livelihood can simply be swept away from under his feet when, as happens more often than you might think, he loses his position at a base and has to start again, with all the efforts of year one going to waste. In other words, it is all very well having a base and customers, but the security of still having it all in the future, with the same conditions that were agreed when accepting the job, is just as important. The geography teacher, though, has both security for the future, and a full wage, and all in year one – a complete contrast to the tennis coach.

If all this is a surprise to you, then you are in for many shocks. There are, in fact, horrendous obstacles often lying in wait for unsuspecting tennis coaches, meaning that they have no alternative but to move on and start again somewhere else. Once the pattern has been established, it is not uncommon for coaches to become thoroughly fed up with it all and leave the profession. They then simply go and look for something else to do in life.

Weekends are usually precious times for coaches, since most adults and all children cannot attend sessions during the daytime from Monday to Friday. This means group coaching is particularly evident at weekends, when a coach is likely to earn most of his money, so imagine the coach arriving at the tennis courts on a Saturday morning as usual, only to find he cannot use them. Apart from the obvious downpour of rain, which nobody can predict, how many other different examples of the sudden unavailability of the coaching court would you like me to list?

Here are just a few, and mainly from my own personal experience: the tennis net is broken or has even been stolen; the tennis net is locked in the shed which nobody can open; the groundsman has put the tennis net up incorrectly, with the net cord cable jammed at one end, and running down to only one foot high at the other net post; the club or sports centre has closed the courts as it is staging a tennis court maintenance weekend, but forgot to inform the coach; there was a storm the previous night and the court is covered in leaves and debris; some youths lobbed beer bottles over the fence late on Friday night, leaving broken glass all over both courts; one of the club teams needs the coaching courts as it has a rearranged match to play, and the captain forgot to inform the coach, or just did not think of informing him that he would have to cancel his coaching; or the coach was informed, but only the night before, causing him more work as he attempts to carry out the impossible task of passing on this news to his customers – although it is less troublesome now with emails and mobile phones, but not much consolation; and when the coach is informed of court unavailability with good notice, the coach's valid objections fall on deaf ears despite the fact that it is his livelihood, affecting many paying customers in the middle of a course, with courts properly booked.

And all these problems, encountered by so many coaches, only occur after they have actually managed to get a court to coach on in the first place, since, unbelievably, this was the number one problem highlighted once in a coaches' survey. Did you ever hear of the schoolteacher unable to teach his pupils because he could not find a classroom?

Not surprisingly, some customers get so fed up with all

the disrupted sessions that they look elsewhere for lessons, or even give up the idea of learning tennis completely.

Another example of a coach losing his Saturday morning teaching time is the common problem of the court being double-booked. The odd thing here is that it always seems to be the person who made the later, or second, booking, who keeps the court, since it is that person's name which now appears on the computerised booking slot, overriding the earlier block booking made in the coach's name.

Common sense should prevail in such a situation and priority for the court be given to the full-time coach, but this rarely happens. The fact that the court has been booked in the coach's name for the last sixteen weeks, and, importantly, affects his salary and many customers, rather than just two casual players having a knockabout, which could easily be rearranged or missed that day with no consequences whatsoever, except for their personal disappointment, seems to make little impression on the duty manager.

Of course, the truth is that the two casual players should not have been able to book the court in the first place, as the court had already been reserved in the coach's name. This double-booking example tends to occur at sports centres, country clubs and indoor centres, although not at all of them, I hasten to add, but it certainly happens more often than you might think.

However, the receptionist, who is at fault for allowing a second or double-booking, not only still gets fully paid that week, but usually is never even aware that he has made such an error. This is because, when the problem arises on the Saturday morning, it is the weekend receptionist now on duty. So it is never the guilty receptionist who takes the criticism, nor do they even know they have caused such disruption, since nobody remembers to tell them on the Monday morning. The result of this shambles is, of course, predictable: they make exactly the same error the following week, and the whole problem sparks off again.

It is funny how the coach is never allowed to reserve a court for a lesson when it is already booked in someone else's name, but when it is the other way round, the chairman or manager of the tennis base deems it perfectly acceptable, especially when the coaching courts are required for a team match.

And if you think these problems are not enough to contend with, how about the almost unthinkable, encountered not only by me, but by several coaches I have spoken to: another coach got there first. As John McEnroe would say: 'You cannot be serious!'. But I most certainly am, as I have stated before in this book. A different coach is actually on the court which was booked in the resident coach's name, and is in the process of coaching his own customers.

And on one occasion, the club captain of an LTA club, with no authorisation whatsoever, had actually started coaching my assistant coach's customers. Perhaps this is why one of the seven commandments in the official manual of a certain coaching organisation states that one cannot coach where another resident professional is employed – a very sensible commandment indeed, but who enforces this rule, because ridiculous incidents like this still occur? And it is no laughing matter when it is your livelihood at stake.

You will be pleased to hear that the committee did support my assistant on this particular occasion, but only after arguing our position over several weeks, and waiting for the decision at the next committee meeting, when it was too late, and after so much disruption had already been caused, with my assistant coach disgruntled for a very long time. And did the club, or the club captain whose fault it was, compensate my full-time assistant for her lost wages? Of course not.

And just consider the working relationship between the club captain, my assistant and me from then on, not to mention how unwelcome newcomers to our coaching course and the tennis club must have felt with such politics going on.

But, if the committee supported me on this occasion, I can assure you that the arrival of a new leisure manager or chairperson at an LTA club can result in a change of coach in an instant. It can be because the new leisure manager favours a friend of his, or because he has found a hobby coach who will offer his services at much lower prices, and will also give the tennis base a greater share of the profits.

The chairperson defends himself after the outcry by claiming he was looking after his members by offering them cheaper coaching, or that, by opening it up to all and sundry, he is giving the members more choice, and making the coaches more competitive. He may well have been in politics in an earlier life – 'more choice', 'more competition'.

I heard of one sudden change of coaches that was due to a dispute between the chairman and the coach over a girlfriend. The chairman had all the power, so it was curtains for the coach, as is always the case if a coach ever dares to challenge any decision made by the one in power.

Do these sorts of incidents ever happen to a schoolteacher? Can you honestly imagine one entering his classroom, only to find another teacher beat him to it that morning, or the desks had been stolen, or the classroom was locked, taking three hours before anyone could gain access? I do not think so. As a young boy at school, I certainly do not remember such goings-on.

However, if such unusual things did ever happen, the teacher would still be paid and would get the full support of the Head, and the pupils would return the following week. And, failing all that, the teacher would have a union to call upon for any unfair treatment.

What a contrast to the tennis coach. No union effectively to look after his interests, and all he gets is an apology from the receptionist or leisure manager, groundsman or team captain, or chairperson or club committee, and no wage that Saturday morning. And a month, or week later, it can all happen again. Worse still, the coach will be lucky if all his customers return, and any support sought from the tennis governing body or coaching organisation, for which the coach has paid his membership dues,is non-existent.

While you would not expect an employed schoolteacher to be treated in such a manner, other self-employed people do not suffer in this way either. You do not hear of the gardener not able to do his Friday work one week because the owners locked the garden gate, or left rubbish strewn across the lawns denying him access to his work. Or a builder, hired to erect large extensions over several months or years, turning up one day to find another builder has decided to take over the work he had started. Nor do such self-employed workers find that, halfway through a job, their pay has been suddenly cut in half. But all this can, and does, happen to tennis coaches!

I am sure that some of the more business-minded among you will be thinking: what about the terms in a coach's contract? What contract? The fact is, many smaller clubs and sports or leisure centres are loath to commit to such a thing. In the case of leisure or sports centres, they have usually never been asked to provide one for the football, netball, squash or trampoline coach, who have all probably taken on their positions in their spare time as a hobby. So the manager is not going to start writing up a contract just for the tennis coach, even if it is his full-time job. It is also not something many managers feel comfortable about, since it has legal ramifications attached to it, which basically frightens them a little, or even a lot.

When addressing some fifty coaches at a seminar once, in my days as the Regional Director for a coaching organisation, I asked how many of them had signed contracts at all the main bases at which they coached. Only a handful had, even though many were running large junior programmes at sports and leisure centres, or at country clubs or in the local park, all without anything in writing. When I enquired if they had encountered problems over arrangements they thought had been agreed, I was bombarded with their horror stories.

When I happen to tell people that surviving as a full-time tennis coach in Great Britain is fraught with difficulties, and can even become virtually impossible, they do not believe me. If I then start going into a few details, they just about begin to understand. However, if I tried to relate all that I have experienced, I would have to stop after a few minutes in order to avoid turning a social situation into the equivalent of reading Dante's *Inferno* out loud, for which I would not be thanked – hence, the 'health warning' given at the beginning of this chapter. Fortunately, in written form, what I am recounting can be taken in small doses and, hopefully, be more convincing for it.

Coming back, then, to the main narrative: some of the examples I have given regarding court loss can, of course, be difficult to include in a contract, such as leaves from an overnight storm covering the courts, but a contract does solve many issues, and, importantly, clarifies what has been agreed in the first place, rather than relying on memory from a verbal discussion. Worse still, and quite commonplace, is when a dispute arises, the person with whom terms were verbally agreed has left, and their replacement just dreams up conditions which suit him at the time. The whole thing is so ad hoc and amateurish that it is little wonder coaches with a genuine desire to be professional are driven away from a career in tennis, or are forced to emigrate in order to carry on doing the job they love.

Interestingly, in the 2006 Blueprint for British tennis there is mention of the need for 'robust coach/club contracts'. Unfortunately, I have yet, in my own experience, to see the fruits of such a proposal. But, even if the coach does have a contract and it has been contravened, presenting it to the leisure centre manager the next day, in an effort to sort things out, can still have dire consequences for him.

On one occasion when I did this, after the tennis courts, clearly booked in my name, were deliberately handed over to a group of hotel guests to allow them to stage an all-day tournament without first consulting me, the manager simply picked up his pen and crossed through the clause of my contract forbidding such action. If I had caused a fuss, I would have been given a month's notice and would have lost my coaching position. When you have a mortgage to pay and family to support, and a comprehensive coaching programme at stake, you think twice before rocking the boat. My contract was, in effect, worthless. But worse still, it ensured that I kept to terms which were of interest to the tennis base, but any for my benefit could simply be discarded if necessary, as indeed they were.

In addition, there is a total lack of support from the LTA for tennis coaches, once they have set out on a coaching career. I do not mean that there is no support in terms of training, job offers, or lectures and guidelines on how to set up your tennis business: the LTA provide well in these areas. But, in many cases, from the job protection point of view, it is quite impossible for most coaches to develop their programmes to a level where they can earn a living without an unreasonable risk of losing it all, through no fault of their own, and with only a few weeks' notice given, if not hours'. The simple truth is the LTA do not cover this area at all.

In taking over at a club from a rather sleepy and disorganised hobby coach once, who barely made an appearance twice a week, I unwittingly started to cause problems by energetically organising many activities on different days. The club, by the way, had never had a full-time coach before. While my customers enjoyed this new and very proactive approach, the committee most certainly did not – in fact, they did not want to see nearly so much of me, or was it that they did not want to see so many juniors occupying their precious courts? Huge problems ensued. The perception was that I was taking valuable court time away from the members, even though I stuck to the allocated coaching court and times of use.

At another club I had to apply to the committee for a one-off extra coaching court I required at an off-peak time. The next committee meeting was ten weeks away, but I was informed that I had to wait, even though, in practical terms, I needed a decision before then. On another occasion, when I was wise to this and applied for extra courts months in advance, I was told by the committee after their meeting: 'Sorry, we ran out of time and did not discuss your extra court request, as there was much argument over the ladies' teas'.

The first problem for tennis coaches is that our bosses seldom appreciate they are dealing with a full-time 'employee' trying to do a professional job. With proper support and well laid-down guidelines from the LTA, however, life would be much easier, safer, and more rewarding. Junior programmes would run smoothly and be far better geared to producing more players of quality, some of whom might even have a realistic chance of getting somewhere. This, in turn, would attract more reliable, hard-working, and level-headed people to follow a tennis coaching career, rather than be scared off.

But the LTA, quite honestly, either do not understand the reality of the situation, or simply cannot be bothered to get involved and sort it out. They may be sympathetic, and even have written guidelines for how coaches should operate at a tennis base, but the fact is they are only guidelines, and however good the advice may be, it is not a standard followed or enforced throughout the tennis industry. So coaches and their managers sit down and draw up their own individual contracts, if one is signed at all, which do not cover the important points I am highlighting, and, in any case, only protect the base rather than the coach.

And, if anything like the Saturday morning fiascos I have just described occur, the LTA, if approached, will state that they 'cannot interfere in private, internal affairs'.

The whole situation is so unsatisfactory and unprofessional that it beggars belief. If the coach's position were set up properly, apart from these ridiculous incidents seldom occurring any more, the LTA would be there to call upon to help sort out disputes of any nature, as a responsible governing body.

Unfortunately, the overwhelming majority of tennis coaches must face the fact that they are very much alone, unless they are lucky enough to be working in really exceptional circumstances. The norm is that coaches have so many uncertainties to contend with, and no means of putting things right, because there is simply nobody to turn to for proper support. It is an unenviable position to be in, and not one on which you can base a career.

In my own case, I resorted to limiting my coaching time at an LTA club in order to avoid creating too much hostility. I then set up elsewhere to allow myself three bases from which to operate, so as to have some insurance, should I lose one of the bases. In effect, the more coaching I set up at a tennis club, the more I sensed resentment, jealousy and bad feeling from the committee, even though my actual coaching had always been praised. To survive at a club, I soon realised that, by limiting my coaching time there, I kept the committee much happier and ensured at least some cooperation from them. Incidentally, I had even been advised to do this by more than one officer of a committee.

But how ridiculous. When the courts were available, and members wanted more coaching. Some of the club members even travelled to my other external bases for coaching, even when it could all have been carried out at their LTA club.

Can you imagine the car salesperson being told to sell fewer cars, or limiting him to three days only in the showroom when customers are making enquiries on more than three days a week, and the salesman is willing to do the extra hours?

As a serious coach, you just have to hope you have the chance to work at a more professionally-run tennis base, like a Performance Centre or a big 'clubmarked' club, but there are still no guarantees even then.

I have known many a committee think it is all right to invite other club members, who happen to be qualified in coaching, to start advertising their coaching services as well. And this is after they have put in place a full-time coach, and when there is hardly enough coaching for one person to do. Those on the committee just do not think it through: they make coaching at their club a free-for-all, believing this is better because it offers choice to their members, and are quite ignorant of the consequences of such an arrangement. With other club members coaching, who are neither full-time coaches nor nearly so well-qualified, they easily undercut the official full-time coach's fees, since whatever they earn is just pin money for them. Do I need to explain the outcome of such an intrusion, and the impact it can have on the unsuspecting and hard-working full-time coach?

Moreover, this new arrangement can be sprung upon the full-time coach in an instant; there have even been examples, as already stated, of coaches turning up to find others already on court doing the coaching; or the coach discovers that someone else's fees are being advertised on the club noticeboard.

Too many committees forget that they are dealing with a full-time professional with a livelihood at stake. All the coach wants is some sensible support and action taken in such situations, but he is constantly pushed to the bottom of the pile and his complaint is considered of little concern. While all these examples of how a full-time coach gets treated may surprise you, it can partly be explained by the sort of people who sometimes serve on committees, especially in the smaller clubs.

What typically happens is the following: the chairperson had to have his arm twisted to take on the role; the secretary is someone who is familiar with administration and good on the computer; a club member is persuaded to act as treasurer because he is an accountant; two ladies take their place because they simply enjoy catering and can do the teas; and others allow themselves to be co-opted because they like to throw their weight around and have their say.

Their ability to run a club for its members is questionable, to say the least: they may not even be regular tennis players, let alone appreciate the needs of a tennis coach, but they still make the decisions.

Such is their ignorance of tennis, they are more likely to think a backhand slice is a slither of ham for the team's tea, and an American tournament is a tennis match played in the USA. When a coaching matter is raised at a committee meeting, they make their decision without investigating further or consulting the coach, and without ever being aware of the consequences of some of their decisions. Is there another occupation where one's livelihood is handled in such an amateurish and totally irresponsible way?

At one tennis club, the committee even allowed an unqualified and unregistered coach to advertise his services – and this when they had already taken on a full-timer. And when someone pointed this out to the committee, one of the officers was instructed to advise this person that he ought to stop.

However, this instruction was ignored by the unqualified coach, and he carried on with the four or five lessons he already had in hand, and no further action was taken. There were, of course, public liability insurance and child protection implications to consider in this case. But this was the only reason the unqualified coach was warned in the first place! And what was the outcome? The club lost its best and only full-time, fully-qualified coach. The problem was that nobody on the committee really cared enough to take proper action and sort it out. It was just a nuisance to the committee which did not directly affect them and something they just hoped would go away, but it was the proper coach who went away, and the committee just shrugged their shoulders as though it could not be helped.

And as I have already pointed out, who does the full-time coach turn to in such a situation? Certainly not the LTA or the coaching organisations to which coaches pay their membership fees, because they too are reluctant to interfere 'in private, internal disputes'.

The outcome, though, is so bad for British tennis, since it is the wrong coach who ends up leaving, and the professional, full-time coach, probably with a family to consider, has to suffer the consequences of a serious loss of income. The juniors at the club then suffer as well, with the continuity of their coaching development suddenly interrupted, and any chances they might have had of fulfilling their potential much affected.

It is also not unheard of for the full-time coach to be expected to join a club, paying full membership before he can coach there. And this is even when the club is so small it cannot provide the coach with a full-time living wage. In such a case I always believe the club should be grateful to have gained the services of a full-time coach, but gratitude is so often in short supply. Does the schoolteacher, working at a private school, have to pay the yearly students' fees before he can start teaching there? Or is the golf pro made to join the golf club where he is the resident professional? I have mentioned this requirement to several friends of mine, who are golf professionals, and they either laugh, or find it too difficult to believe.

I have often wondered why the approach towards tennis coaches by managers and committees is so different.

Tennis coaches seem to be put in a category of their own, and those with power over them simply seem to be intent on making their working life as difficult as possible. When I once stayed on after coaching to join in a club mix-in – it made the numbers even – a letter was received by the committee the next day complaining that I was not a full-paying member of the club.

This is another example of how tennis bases will do their utmost to extract as much money from a coach as possible, when any coach is effectively offering his professional services to a club for free, and is usually the club's best vehicle to attract new members, and also the person in the best position to retain existing members.

A good example of this was when I heard how a local village club, with a small membership, invited a full-time coach to develop junior coaching on Saturday mornings, around the turn of the century. The coach worked hard to attract many new juniors, enabling him to form three groups of between six to eight children, which meant he had £70 to £100 coming in for his morning's work. When, the following year, the new chairperson decided the club should benefit from the coach's hard-earned income and levied a £50 fee on him for what he did every Saturday with the juniors, when no payment had been requested before, the coach naturally complained. He had, of course, no chance of winning the argument with the committee, so he left.

The conclusion that has to be reached is that some committees are not only clueless, but are capable of wreaking untold havoc in British tennis. How can anyone not recognise the unfairness of such a dramatic change in the financial agreement that was initially made with the coach? And this is without acknowledging the early work and marketing he carried out, singlehandedly introducing enough juniors into the club to make his morning's coaching worthwhile. In many respects, the committee should have offered him a retainer for increasing their membership and being prepared to offer his services to such a small club when he was a full-timer.

But the committee stuck to their guns, as always seems to be the case, since the decision had been made and they cannot ever be seen to be wrong and to have acted irresponsibly. The club promptly lost the only full-time coach they were ever likely to have, and the junior coaching programme collapsed. It was not only a disaster for the club and its juniors, who were enjoying their coaching and making good progress, but does anyone, in such a case, ever consider the dire consequences for the coach?

Despite paying membership fees to three bodies – his coaching organisation, the BTCA (British Tennis Coaches' Association) and the LTA – the coach had absolutely nobody to turn to for support. With the possible loss of some individual lessons at the village club as well, the coach would have gone home to report to his wife that the family income had just been reduced by around £200 per week. And he had not done anything wrong. In fact, it was because he had done so much that was right, and put into place a new Saturday junior coaching programme, exactly as the club had requested, that he ended up having to leave. He then had to put in extra time and effort to increase coaching at his other bases, or find another club.

I happen to know that this particular coach, who was very hard-working and organised, sadly ended up leaving the profession he had been happy in for many years after another similar incident occurred elsewhere. Where does the coach find another base in his area at which to coach? It is not easy.

A very common charge imposed upon the tennis coach is for court hire. But when this is implemented at a club where members do not pay for courts, then why should members, who have already paid their subscription, be charged inflated coaching fees to cover what the coach has to pay extra for the court?

With such a rule, the coach feels much less welcome, and some resentment is felt all round, with members who take lessons effectively paying twice for the court, and the coach reluctantly having to increase his fees as well to cover his court hire.

There are far better ways to raise revenue from the coach, which do not interfere with the harmony of the club, such as asking him to give a free introduction to tennis for juniors and adults for two hours a week during the summer months.

Here is the story of another proactive, full-time coach.

Having secured his position as a club's resident coach, he worked wonders attracting many four to seven year-olds on to his programme. Halfway through, the chairman instructed the coach not to allow any of the twenty children to continue unless they had paid their annual membership fee. This is yet another example of moving the goalposts without prior consultation, since this had not been a requirement at the start. The children had nothing else they could attend or make use of at the club, and, in addition, a great link had been formed with the local primary school thanks to this particularly proactive coach.

Why do clubs deliberately impose rules which dissuade children from taking up tennis, and make their coach's life more difficult, when they should be encouraging all and sundry? As long as actual members were offered places on the course first, it is much better for the club, the junior members and the coach if non-members are allowed to attend and therefore increase the numbers and secure the viability of the class. But it is impossible trying to explain this to a chairman who has already made his mind up, and wants, anyway, to feel that he has a controlling influence over the coach.

If only he could stop to consider what would happen if he decided to take a golf lesson at his local golf club, he might act differently. He would not be asked to pay a joining fee and annual golf subscription before receiving a lesson. And yet, as an adult golf member, he could easily enjoy all the other facilities, including the bar, but still the golf club would not expect him to join for just attending his weekly lesson. At the tennis club, in this instance, we were dealing with under-8s, who gain nothing for being members, and indeed only attend in most cases because their mothers think it is a good idea, and take them along. Five to seven year-olds do not use the other facilities on offer, order a meal and a pint at the bar, or enjoy their own arranged, casual game of tennis in between lessons.

The outcome was that the coach could not change the chairman's mind on this issue, so this part of his coaching programme collapsed, and it was not long before the coach resigned, having realised his relationship with the chairman had been irretrievably damaged.

And where is this proactive coach now? Probably following an alternative career, and who can blame him? So another loss to British tennis, as well as the twenty children who were also presumably lost as they went off to pursue a different activity. How can the LTA sit back and allow one individual to make such poor decisions in one of their affiliated clubs, affecting young children being introduced to tennis, and allow a good coach to be lost?

My co-author knows of a relatively young, hard-working

and quite experienced coach at a Performance Centre who is planning to take up another profession as soon as he passes the relevant exams. The simple reason for this is that he cannot see any real future in being a tennis coach. And there is yet another coach, again quite experienced, at the same Centre, equally able to make a useful contribution to British tennis, who is contemplating moving over to teaching golf because the set-up is far more professional.

I do, however, have a solution to all this by introducing a three-way coaches' contract which I shall explain more fully later in the book: if implemented, it would never allow the sort of incidents I have described to occur. The coach would then be completely protected and supported, and able to concentrate on providing a very professional service, which is how it should be. Coaches could then sleep more easily at night, as they would no longer be at the mercy of the whims and ways of new managers and chairpersons. I myself remember sleepless nights only too well.

Indelibly etched in my brain is the sleepless night I endured following this whim from a chairman: having set up one hour of adult, and four and a half hours of junior, group coaching, plus three to five individual lessons at a village club each week, I was asked to attend an autumn committee meeting where it was announced that, after careful consideration, the club felt I should offer my first seven lessons of every week free of charge. This was not in the original agreement, but was believed to be fair and right for the club and its coach, and was to start from the following year.

I had to go back and explain that I only did up to ten hours' coaching at each of my three bases, and, if the other two bases imposed something similar, then I would be working for free. Thankfully, there was one committee member with some common sense, who had been absent for the original discussion of the proposal. He reacted angrily on my behalf and, in effect, made the committee shelve the idea. Much to my relief, and that of my wife and children, life continued as before.

I did warn you not to be surprised as I reveal what happens, sadly, much too often, to tennis coaches as they try to forge a career for themselves. All these examples of how some tennis coaches are treated are real. Nothing is exaggerated.

So here we go again.

As the official coach at one LTA club, my contract forbade me from coaching after 6 pm on any weekday, did not allow any individual coaching at all, and, if it rained for my 'ladies' morning' class, we all got soaked because I was not trusted to hold a clubhouse key, and the car park was over two hundred yards away. Another example, then, of the committee obviously thinking that these were reasonable terms for a full-time coach trying to earn a living. Such regulations hardly make one feel welcome, either.

I have to take the blame for such terms, of course, because, while I obviously did not agree with them, I did sign the contract in order to secure the job, and just hoped I could persuade the committee to change these ridiculous conditions for the following year. I had taken over mid-term from a part-time coach who had previously accepted, and worked to, the same rules. No wonder he gave up, and he was only part-time. But what else could I do? There was not another tennis club around the corner needing a coach.

Despite my co-author's horror at so many examples being included – it goes against his notions of style – I am doing so in order to give you a proper insight into the trials and tribulations of the profession. Who would ever start on a tennis coaching career knowing that this is the reality? Are skilled people treated so poorly in any other walk of life?

The schoolteacher does not have any of these problems to contend with, but, should he choose to leave the school where he teaches, he even has the advantage of applying for a job in a good number of schools within easy driving distance. Not so with the tennis coach. He almost certainly has to move house, disturb his children's education, and cause his wife to lose or disrupt her job too, as there are few local tennis clubs to approach in any one area. And he will be lucky if one of the local clubs in his area happens to be searching for a new coach at the time he needs a new position.

It must be difficult for you, the reader, to believe most of these revelations, and you may wonder what can be done to change matters to support the full-time coach, but I do have a solution, as I have indicated before, and it can be so easily implemented.

The three-way contract that I propose later on in the book would solve so much, protecting the coach, customers and tennis base, and avoid the following situation which prompted one of the best coaches I know in the UK to leave his large commercial tennis centre.

At that time, for groups, he was paid £14 per hour from a total of £32 collected by the centre. When the fees were increased, giving the centre £36 per hour, all they allowed the coach from this increase was an extra 20p!

As the coach said, it was an insult too far, and he left. Of course, his customers had their tennis development disrupted, the centre probably lost the best coach they had ever had, or are likely to have, but did they care, or even realise how good this particular person was? And if the coach left to pursue a different profession, which he may well have done with justification, here is yet another great loss to British tennis. But nobody does anything about it. And on his own, what can the coach do? All the LTA would say, if asked, would be: 'We cannot interfere with internal decisions or disputes'.

My co-author knows of a very well-known indoor commercial centre, where the highly-qualified tennis coaches, all of whom reached at least county standard during their playing careers, have to pay the first £600 they earn every month to the centre – over £7,000 a year for the privilege of trying to earn a living there. This is not to say that coaches should not pay a reasonable rent to work at such a base, but when the coaches are dictated to in terms of: other work they are expected to do; times they must coach; courts not always available for them; fees they must charge; and importantly, a full working week which is difficult to achieve because too many coaches are taken on by the centre, providing the owner, of course, with an extra £7,000 each time!, then one can understand why they are unhappy about their terms. In addition, on top of the rent the coaches religiously pay the centre, a court fee is still applied as well. So it is not always a bed of roses at bigger clubs either. One does wonder how motivated these coaches are when taking the mini tennis classes that are part of the club's function as a Performance Centre.

In another example of disputes over coaching fees, the Head of PE at a private school had agreed for my assistant coach to be paid £12 per half-hour, divided equally among up to six pupils. Everyone was more than happy, and a successful year-round coaching programme was run on outdoor courts, with some lessons in curriculum time. All was fine until a new Head of PE was appointed who wanted the coaching to continue, but summoned my assistant to a meeting in mid-September to inform him that his fees were too high: £7 was to be the new half-hour rate with immediate effect.

But, much to the new PE teacher's surprise, despite my assistant arguing his case, and with my support, I might add, the only thing that happened with immediate effect was that my assistant and I, resigned.

You have to wonder how the PE teacher would react if she were told, after working successfully and with a full programme for a year, that her wage would now be cut by nearly half. Although this very point was made, coupled with the fact that there had been no complaints about the fees according to the previous Head of PE, the new incumbent had already made her decision – it was £7 or nothing. With so many inevitable gaps in the daily coaching programme, it was only just worthwhile the coach taking the job on at £12 per half-hour. So walking away was the only option, and the school never did replace the coach. Ironically, he had considered asking for a small rise before the start of the new academic year, but had decided not to.

It seems to me that the situation described above would not occur in any other full-time profession: what is it that we tennis coaches have done to deserve such treatment?

In my own career, I too remember a base I was once forced to leave because a new manager drastically changed the terms of my contract quite out of the blue. I had built up a really substantial junior and adult coaching programme, which brought customers to his leisure complex through my coaching. The new manager decided that he should take over the setting of my coaching fees and keep a huge percentage, rather than charge me merely for court and floodlight hire, as had been the arrangement up to then. The effect was a halving of my income. Despite my willingness to compromise and take a small pay reduction, the new manager stood his ground, so again the inevitable happened.

Quite frankly, it was a huge loss to the leisure complex, since the manager was never able to replace me, so the complete tennis programme, which was substantial, collapsed. I was later reliably informed that the manager did not particularly care. From his point of view, there was far more money in the attached hotel business and in the staging of conferences for him to worry about the relatively small income lost for the leisure club if the tennis coach departed. But why did he not have the sense to realise my worth and keep me on, or recall me? He could have kept a successful tennis section as well. Other than casual court bookings, I had run the tennis side single-handedly for him, so it was all financial gain for his leisure complex. I still cannot understand why he chose to lose it all. But he had made his decision and there was nothing anyone could do about it, even though many of my customers spoke up for me.

This is another example of how too often, once the person in charge has made his decision, there is no going back – it is usually too embarrassing for them. I should point out that this sort of incident – so catastrophic for the full-time coach, i.e. me, in this instance – could not happen if my three-way contract solution were in place.

Continuing with the litany – the word is my co-author's suggestion: I would prefer to call it something else, but I do not have his vocabulary or literary background – here are four more experiences I think you will find revealing and interesting, and, in a perverse way, you may even enjoy reading about them, unless, of course, you are thinking of becoming a tennis coach!

By complete chance, while holidaying in Spain, I bumped into a tennis coach who invited me to a soirée at his house. There I met twelve British coaches who were all doing well, and they asked why I did not also leave Britain to coach abroad. 'Why do you think I should?' I said. One of them replied: 'Don't you know?' So I tentatively answered: 'The weather?'. And, in complete unison, all twelve coaches shouted: 'No, committees!'. It was very early coaching days for me during that Spanish trip, but, after the last twenty years or so, I now realise only too well how right they were.

They went on to recount the many bad experiences they had had in Great Britain, all very similar to those I have already described, and am about to describe in the next few paragraphs. Quite simply, they had been driven out of the UK by tennis club committees and forced to set up base in Spain. The truth is that the twelve coaches in question were the sort that British tennis could ill afford to lose: they were enthusiastic, proactive and had initiative – so much so that they were not prepared to tolerate conditions that all too frequently still prevail in the UK. They just upped sticks and went to a better place.

An estate agent friend, quite new to the tennis club where I was the coach, was co-opted on to the committee one year. It was not long before the tennis coach's activities were discussed at one of the first committee meetings he attended. A few days later I happened to see him in the street.

'Steve,' he called over to me, 'I couldn't believe how you just sat there the other night, taking such nonsense spoken about your coaching.'

'Don't worry,' I explained, 'I'm used to it. They just have

to have their little dig and moan at me, even when they know I've done nothing wrong. It makes them feel more in control, and keeps me on my guard. Most of what they say is nothing but hot air, and it all gets forgotten quite quickly, because there is no substance to any of their comments.'

The estate agent looked quite bewildered and responded with: 'If the chairperson walked into my estate agency and started dictating to me how I should work, telling me how many houses I could display, how to advertise, for how long and for how much, I'd tell him where to go. What a nerve they've got!'.

Of course, he was right. However, the reason coaches do not react as my friend might have, but just sit there and suffer in silence, is because they have become accustomed to such treatment, and realise it is best to concentrate on only reacting when something actually comes up which is likely to have a serious effect on their programmes. In any case, if the coach wants a job, what else can he do? He ends up coming to the conclusion that he is likely to get the same treatment wherever he goes. The story of the twelve British coaches in Spain is eloquent testament to that. I shall always remember a new, very supportive chairperson having a quiet word with me after such a committee meeting as described above. 'Don't worry about some of the comments you hear,' she said. 'You must have sleepless nights over them sometimes. It's just the committee's way of managing you. They know you are a very good coach, but, because you do so much, they just like to feel they are staying in control and keeping you on a tight rein. There's a lot of jealousy, because they see you enjoying yourself earning money at what they consider to be their club. They just don't understand.'

What happened to the fine words of the LTA Blueprint of 2006?: 'We will help clubs to see coaches as an opportunity rather than a threat'.

And the chairperson was right to have a word with me, making sure I was not upset by the various jibes that were made, rather than allowing me to try and argue with a whole group of committee members, most of whom were retired and socialised together, with the tennis club, and all the gossip, as their main topic of conversation each week. The chairperson will never realise just how comforting her words had been to me at the time.

If you can bear it, there is more. But, if you want a little rest, I shall quite understand.

One full-time coach was forced to walk down a lane to a house to ask for the key from an elderly lady in order to gain access to the club courts. The committee would not allow him his own key, but assured him that the elderly lady was always in. By having to return the key afterwards, unless he could pass it on to other members who had come to play, the coach always had to allow for an extra twenty minutes for a one-hour lesson.

At this juncture, I would like to ask the following pertinent questions: how can a professional run his business based on an elderly lady always being in? Does this practice occur in any other line of work?

My proposed contract would avoid such an absurd problem, and many others as well.

One coach I know has a very clever ruse to protect himself against outrageous committee decisions which might affect his day-to-day work: his mother! What she did was apply to become a committee member solely to be sure that she was 'in the know', and importantly, there at the time any terrible accusations happened to be flying around at the meetings regarding her son. She was then in a position to influence any subsequent decisions which could threaten his livelihood. At the time of writing, all was going well apparently, with one or two potentially unpleasant situations having been avoided through her presence. But what a way to gain some security.

Tennis clubs, and in particular smaller tennis clubs, just want to be able to say they are doing their bit for the juniors, and therefore British tennis, by allowing coaching, but with minimal disruption to the adults' requirements. And, for the smaller clubs, taking on a hobby coach best fits the bill. By having a coach with less time on his hands, who does not organise many activities, with few demands and cheaper fees, there is little interference in what goes on at the club, and less chance of upsetting members. They think that everyone is happy, including the coach, because he has already completed a full working week in his main profession, so hardly wants to do much more anyway.

Of course, everyone believes it is all hunky-dory, with the important exception of the talented eight year-old, who, if only he or his parents knew it, might have been able to make better progress in the sport if a professional and more comprehensive coaching programme had been in place. In such a situation the youngster's chances of any serious success are simply non-existent, as it is often at the smaller clubs that a talented junior's tennis career will begin.

The truth is that the more proactive a coach is, the more problems and headaches he creates for himself. In the end, his sanity is severely tested, unless he accepts the stark reality of the situation and stops being so ambitious, but this means, in effect, that he will have to give up the idea of being a full-time coach because he simply cannot create enough work for himself.

At one coaches' seminar I was discussing junior squad coaching fees with a hobby coach. At the time I charged £5 an hour, with just under £4 being the national average, following a coaching organisation's survey. The hobby coach in question, however, was only allowed to charge £2.50 by his club. 'I bet you'd double your fees if you were coaching full-time,' I joked. 'Steve,' he immediately retorted, 'if I were full-time like you, I'd treble my fees.' And he was perfectly serious.

I make this point because every chairperson has a completely different view about fees, which in some cases has led to coaches resigning. This particular hobby coach could never have changed to full-time because the committee had set his fees too low. I can just imagine the fireworks at the committee meeting if he turned up to announce he had become full-time and wanted to treble the amount he had been charging. His customers would also have complained, of course, as they would if the hobby coach left and were replaced by a full-timer with higher fees, which is not an unusual occurrence in LTA clubs.

This is exactly the position I was once in, taking over from a hobby coach and only able to risk setting my fees 25% higher, and I still could not earn the national average wage. Such clubs put themselves in the position of never being able to take on a full-time coach because of their fee structure having always been set around the hobby coach. And do not be alarmed at the aforementioned hobby coach's apparent greed. He was quite right to realise he could not become full-time, I can assure you: he had already worked out that he could never earn a decent living.

The problem with the coaching organisation's survey, with just under £4 national average findings, was that it did not state what percentage of respondents were hobby, part-time or full-time coaches. Again, my three-way contract solution would stop any disputes ever brewing in the first place, and would educate amateur committees about professional coaching requirements, so that just guessing at fees and conditions would become a thing of the past.

And what always has to be considered is the following: as soon as there is one conflict between the coach and the committee, it unfortunately tends to spill into other coaching matters to the detriment of the coach and his customers.

Still on the subject of coaches' fees, in the 1990s the LTA did produce guidelines for what a customer should expect to pay for a one-hour individual lesson. They were: £18, £15 and £12, depending on the coach's 3-Level LTA qualification. But these were abandoned when there were so many complaints from coaches. A wise move in my opinion, since I worked out that, based upon the £15 figure, for the average outdoor tennis coach it was almost impossible to earn £10,000 a year after expenses.

So, in 1995, unless you were happy to live below the poverty line, you certainly needed to change profession, or be prepared to work long hours, or find with difficulty, a thriving indoor centre that did not charge you a lot for the privilege of working there. Or you might have considered becoming a golf pro, because, in the 1990s, golf pro fees were on average more than double those of the LTA's guidelines. And that is when the golf pro is not affected by rain, nor does he have the same ball expense of a tennis coach, and he probably saves considerably on time and money by not needing to travel around as much as the typical tennis coach.

One coach I know will confirm these figures and has put up with his lowly income for thirty years. But he is single and still lives at home with his parents. He just accepts that he will never be able to buy his own house, and prefers to coach rather than do a better-paid job he would not enjoy. He is still in the same situation today.

And when a coach goes to work in a school because it may seem the ideal way to attract new customers and, at the same time, earn some more revenue, it can sometimes turn out to be more of a problem than it is worth. The success of coaching in a school invariably relies upon the member of staff coordinating it all for you. If they are less than enthusiastic about tennis, and not efficient or reliable into the bargain, the school tennis programme will probably not get off the ground, even though there are plenty of pupils wanting to attend.

I once approached a private school with a view to starting after-school tennis coaching, but the PE teacher turned me down. One term later, however, the History teacher, a keen tennis and hockey player herself, contacted me and arranged as much coaching as I could handle at the time.

On many occasions, in fact, I have heard how a coach has been informed that there was not enough interest when, in truth, he would have been oversubscribed.

This happened to me at a school where I had been established for a number of years, with a waiting list for my coaching every summer, but I was informed in the January by the newly appointed PE teacher that the tennis would not be viable that year owing to a lack of demand.

It just demonstrates how insecure every tennis programme is for the self-employed tennis coach. So, apart from regular work being lost for a genuine reason, such as loss of facilities, timetable changes, or lack of interest, coaches are susceptible to losing work when there are no obstacles, and the school coaching programme has been thriving, and still would be if the contact person had taken the appropriate action to organise it.

At a school where the eight-week coaching course was set up immediately after lessons on Mondays, 80% of the class did not turn up the first week because the coordinator had forgotten to remind the pupils about it following the Easter holidays; two of the next three Monday sessions were lost because of bank holidays; and then I was informed that my next two visits had to be cancelled due to a special school event all the students had to attend, which again the coordinator had forgotten about when the arrangements for the course had been made the term before.

At another school, on a similar eight-week summer course, the tennis coaching had to be abandoned after week three due to the excessive noise created alongside the sports hall, which was now being used for GCSE and A level examinations.

And you can guess who suffers when these sorts of incidents occur, when none of it is the fault of that person. The tennis coach also has little chance of replacing the work with alternative coaching when the summer term has begun, but has still spent considerable time on all the preparations for the entire course which has now been interrupted, if not abandoned. In addition, the coach does not get paid, and loses the chance to encourage the pupils to move on to his main tennis base for further coaching. And yet, all the problems could, and should, have been anticipated by the school coordinator, but all the coach ever gets is a verbal apology as he arrives to an empty class, as though it could not have been avoided, and the school promptly cancels the remainder of the course without another thought.

There are also other aspects to be considered: on top of the time spent travelling to and from a school for possibly only a forty-five minute paid session, it is usual for the coach to be expected to clear the hall before coaching, and put the cleared items back in place afterwards on his own. Many a time a coach will have spent up to an extra half an hour preparing the school hall for the lesson, and again afterwards to make sure the school hall is left as he found it. It is a real bonus when preparation time is no more than five minutes for each session, which it can and should be, and when the coach is at least treated with some seriousness and respect.

If you added up the actual number of hours spent for the wage earned for a school course, it would often amount to very little indeed, so coaches have to weigh up very carefully the overall advantages before making such a commitment.

How can the LTA encourage a sensible, hard-working, middle-aged family man to have a career in tennis coaching with such obstacles to overcome? 'Go and get a proper job where you are treated fairly', ought to be the only advice. I only mention these incidents because they are commonplace, and are part and parcel of the reality of tennis coaching.

The harsh world I am describing is simply a million miles away from the frankly cosy world of those who work at the National Tennis Centre in Roehampton. I do offer a solution to all of this, as I have already said, and it is my considered opinion that the governing body of British tennis should take serious notice of my proposals. I also hope that they take serious notice of this book – it is not something that my co-author and I have dashed off on a rainy afternoon when we had nothing else to do.

I am fully aware, of course, that there are other professions which are not exactly plain sailing either, but I hope it is becoming more than evident that there are very serious issues which need to be addressed, otherwise how can we expect anyone to consider a career in tennis coaching? I do not believe there is any other job where life is made quite so difficult for the full-timer. As a colleague frequently reminds me, it seems the tennis coach is always the lowest priority. And sad to say, one has seriously to question whether some tennis club members actually do not want their coach to be successful in getting people playing and making progress, and, in the process, creating a great ambiance. But the good news is that, if my proposed three-way contract were implemented, disgruntled and jealous club members would simply not be able adversely to affect the work of the tennis coach any more in the way that they do now.

If the LTA want to attract and keep the right people in coaching, they need to take action, but I honestly do not believe that they are aware of how badly many coaches are treated. Once again, it is a reality issue, which, as you may have noticed, is a recurring theme of this book. If there is no action taken, or protection provided, tennis coaching in smaller clubs will be increasingly done by hobby coaches, for whom earning enough money to live on and security are not so crucial. But hobby coaches will be less likely to be able to run good junior programmes in the way that committed full-timers can. Without being disrespectful to many hard-working and conscientious hobby coaches, it is my opinion that we actually need as high a percentage as possible of dedicated, full-time professional coaches in order to have a realistic chance of producing better quality players.

How can it be right that good British tennis coaches leave the UK to work in Spain because they know that there is no redress for the treatment handed out to them by club committees? I have also known some very intelligent players of a high standard – and also hard-working and conscientious – who would have liked to take up tennis coaching as a career, but were only too well aware of the perils and huge uncertainties of the job, so they did not dare start. Others did start, but found the politics overwhelming, and were out of it again within a very short space of time.

In golf, I am told, they do not lose their teaching professionals in the way that we do in tennis, nor do schools have such problems either with their teachers.

If you have concluded from reading this book thus far that there is a distinct, and damaging, lack of professionalism in certain areas of British tennis, then you are not far wrong.

And there is more.

The interview for the position of tennis coach can be another trying episode in a coach's life. While the advertising of the post is often done very professionally, the interview itself frequently leaves a lot to be desired, to say the least. I have discussed with golf professionals and schoolteachers, two similar professions to tennis coaching, how the best, or most appropriate, candidate is selected, and the process in these two professions is so completely different from what often happens in tennis.

For the sake of fairness, I should point out that many of the top coaching positions at big clubs or large organisations are conducted quite well, but at smaller clubs, and may I remind you that this book is very much about what happens at the bottom of British tennis, some of the interviews I have been subjected to, or have been told about, are a complete shambles. Here are some examples to end this lengthy but very important chapter.

At one interview the chairman of an LTA tennis club was accompanied by the junior organiser. After the customary introduction and welcome, he passed the lead immediately to his female companion. The surprise on the lady's face said it all, as she looked squarely back at the chairman with the comment: 'Oh, my goodness, I was expecting you to conduct the interview – I don't know what to ask.' And the three of us sat there in silence for what seemed like an eternity, but was probably only about thirty seconds. I just smiled, and upon realising that neither was about to get the interview under way, decided to take control myself. I suggested that I might start by asking them some basic questions about the club, courts, memberships, current coaching set-up, future plans and improvements, and any special requirements they had in mind for the incoming coach. It would have been helpful if either of them could have answered most of my questions without obviously guessing. When I told a friend about this farcical interview, she waggishly enquired whether I had given myself the job.

At another interview, when I was offered the coaching position, I asked when I might expect to receive a contract with the terms we had just discussed. 'Oh, I hadn't considered that,' came the reply from the startled chairperson, who immediately admitted that he had no intention of offering me anything in writing.

When basic questions about the club, or coaching requirements, cannot be answered, or a signed written agreement provided, how can a serious coach consider taking up the position? It just demonstrates how naïve and amateurish committees are, and, do not forget – because they certainly do – they dealing with a person's livelihood! In all honesty, are there any other professions which suffer from such shambolic procedures? I, for one, do not know of any.

However well or badly the formal(!) interview is conducted, it is not unusual for the candidate to be asked to carry out a practical coaching demonstration as well. I personally believe that this on-court test should always be requested, but, having said that, it is at present a waste of time. How can a committee judge one coach against another when they have no idea what constitutes a good tennis lesson?

Despite interviewers not being in a position to judge, they still stand there observing the lesson, and then make a decision affecting several coaches' careers. The one who gets the juniors running madly round the court the most, shouting the loudest, with lots of praise, cracking jokes, and finishing with a fun competition that raises a cheer from all the youngsters, is almost certain to be judged as the best. I say this because I have been a witness to it several times, apart from being amongst it all as one of those interviewed.

The tennis interview, then, is usually a lottery, when it should be the only means a coach has of convincing the interviewers that he is the best, and deserves the job. In other professions, if you demonstrate that you are the best, the interviewers will recognise this, as they are usually experts in the field for the position being offered, so you have a deserved head start over the other candidates. It seldom works out like that in tennis, with the coach's playing standard being the main criterion for choosing one candidate over another. But I can assure you that playing and coaching are definitely not the same thing – in fact, they are poles apart. A high-level player does not necessarily coach well, and a high-level coach does not necessarily play well.

My first lady assistant demonstrated this perfectly when she applied to be Head Coach at a big tennis club. When

I heard that one of the male applicants had been a top county player, I told her that she did not stand a chance, even though we both knew that the strong county player was not nearly as knowledgeable about coaching as she was. With my assistant never having reached county level as a player, and also with the added disadvantage of being female, the interviewing committee were likely only to have eyes for the strongest player among the applicants, and, sure enough, the strongest player, the county-standard candidate, was appointed.

I personally would have offered the position to my lady assistant, because, after all, the job was for a coach, and not a player. But the committee were quite incapable of judging coaching ability, and, what is more, my assistant has encountered this problem time and time again in her career. In fact, she has never managed to secure for herself the higher coaching position she deserves.

A few basic coaching questions from me, when I have been part of the interviewing process on behalf of a club, have always been a very good indication of a coach's on-court ability, which would never have been highlighted during most interviews for a tennis coach. In the next chapter, called 'Coaching', you will read about the reactions of a couple of coaches during the on-court interviews I gave them.

You do have to wonder how we can expect tennis coaches, working within these shores, to be professional and hard-working, and to do the best job possible in looking after and guiding our promising youngsters, when they often have to endure such difficult working conditions. They have so many obstacles to overcome, and constant worries and stress to contend with – all resulting from the thoroughly unsatisfactory situation in which they find themselves. For many it is a matter of survival, doing what will keep them in the job, and, at the same time, making sure they can earn enough money to live on, without upsetting the powers that be, rather than concentrating on what they should be doing for the benefit of their customers, whether they be young, old, or in between.

At one tennis club, where I was taken on as the only qualified tennis coach to do just one weekday morning and one weekend afternoon of coaching, I asked, after a year or so, if I might coach on a couple of evenings as well, since the demand was clearly there and the court space was available. When there was resentment at this request from the committee, my wife was quick to ensure that I did not press them for it again, and told me just to stick to the two sessions that had been agreed, in order that I did not lose the valuable work I already had at this smaller LTA club. She was right – it worked, and I remained there for several more years.

But what about the aspiring juniors who wanted and needed more attention? They obviously did not get it, and probably went off to try out a different sport, or just concentrated on their academic studies, giving up any dreams of ever being good enough to play at Wimbledon.

Do French, Spanish, or German junior club members have this problem of only being allowed one session per week with the coach?

And remember: this was at a small LTA club with no more than five courts, of which there are many in the UK. In order to overcome such a problem now, a junior would have to have tennis-connected parents who were in the know and prepared to take him to a bigger club, or even a Performance Centre, perhaps some distance away, where the fees for a junior programme would be considerably more than those charged by the smaller, local club. Quite frankly, programmes for all, no matter what their background, should be in place at every tennis club in the country, and no impediments allowed to exist for a keen and enterprising coach to set them up.

As I have said before, no wonder Tony Hawks founded TFF (Tennis For Free) in local parks, to the exclusion of LTA clubs. Now, believe it or not, the LTA are finally swarming all over our parks, offering free tennis, resurfacing courts and painting them in attractive colours. I am sure Tony Hawks will be nodding in gobsmacked approval.

Coming back to my own experiences as a full-time coach trying to earn a living, I was fortunate in having positions at several bases, so I was not desperate for increased income from the aforementioned unsupportive tennis club, but another full-time coach may have needed to expand, and, indeed, may have been expecting to, in order to make ends meet.

Here again is a perfect example of what happens: the coach does little and therefore gets on well at his base – no problems arise; the coach is very proactive and is therefore frowned upon – members of the club and the committee become upset and the coach is soon shown the exit door.

In ending this important chapter about the lamentable way many coaches are treated, it is only fair to recognise that some coaches do not always act very professionally themselves. Efficiency, reliability and commitment are three qualities that are sadly lacking sometimes. But, apart from the fact that in all walks of life there are always going to be a few bad eggs, there are certainly many dedicated and conscientious coaches out there working in British tennis. And how desperately we need quality to get out of the mess we are in.

I hope it is obvious for you, the reader, and for the LTA, that something needs to be done. My proposed three-way coaches' contract, explained fully in Chapter 12, would, I believe, go a long way to making tennis coaching an attractive and secure full-time profession. It would also help to turn around some of the less committed coaches, perhaps, by guaranteeing them better treatment in their place of work. The 'robust coach/club contracts' of the 2006 Blueprint, together with the aim of making everything 'professional like golf', might even become reality.

With full-time, well-trained coaches teaching and inspiring throughout British tennis, starting right from the grass roots – community centres, parks, small clubs – upwards, we have more than a chance of success.

CHAPTER 11

Coaching

If in Chapter 9 'Being a Coach', we were approaching the heart of the mess that exists in British tennis, we are now right at the centre of that heart. Quintessentially, 'Coaching' is what this book is all about. This is the true problem of British tennis.

Over the years quite a few pundits have indeed referred to coaching in the UK as being at least a contributory factor in the dearth of British players in the top 100. However, although they have used expressions like 'mediocre at best' to describe it and question its quality, they have never come up with suggestions as to how to improve it. This, in a nutshell, is what I am offering: a solution to the problem, as well as a serious questioning of what goes on now, and has gone on for such a long time.

As I have mentioned before, my route into tennis coaching was very different from that of most coaches, and has given me a very useful, and perhaps unique, vantage point, from which I have been able to see things with a clarity not afforded to those with more conventional credentials.

Firstly, I qualified as a table tennis coach; I then reached county standard in tennis, as I did in table tennis, without ever having taken lessons; subsequently, I gained coaching qualifications in the sport of tennis from three different organisations; not satisfied, I picked the brains of as many famous and well-known tennis coaches as I could find; I also conducted my own research into the game, enabling me to come up with a system and method that I realised were completely missing in British tennis. I honestly believe that I am in a better position than most to see what needs to be done.

As stated in the 'IMPORTANT NOTE' at the beginning of the last chapter, everything you are about to read is true and has actually happened, and comes from my experiences as a grass-roots coach of more than twenty- five years' standing.

Also as in the last chapter, I am providing, for the convenience, and sanity, of the reader, a summary of the many, many examples given of coaching that leaves something, or usually a lot, to be desired.

SUMMARY

Coaches are not trained how to coach properly by the LTA because the LTA do not know! The other two main coaching organisations in the UK are also weak with their training, and even weaker with their examining. During the short time that I stepped in as an examiner for one of the organisations, there was one occasion when I wanted to fail at least four candidates, but not only did they pass with good marks – they were already officially qualified and simply wanted to upgrade to a higher level.

All coaches are left to dream up their own coaching methods, as I had to, with few getting it right, and most believing that coaching is just about encouragement and working juniors hard with various drills, since this is what they went through once as promising juniors themselves, and then had the same approach instilled into them during their own training when becoming coaches.

The accreditation courses they have to attend confuse them further, with content that is mostly irrelevant and boring, and, without a sound coaching method and system to fall back on, it is very difficult for them to know how to use any newly learnt knowledge anyway .

When coaches produce star juniors who win county titles in their age group, they believe that they have contributed greatly to their success. The truth is, though, these stars are just talented and determined juniors who are playing more tennis than most, and who are up against other, less talented players who are also not reaching the standard they ought to through poor coaching. I myself did little for Giles Davey – British under-18 Parks Champion; John Shephard – winner on the professional Futures Tour; and Tim Wilcher – voted number 1 out of 10,000 hopefuls in the Cliff Richard 'Search for a Star' initiative. All three were multi-talented, needing minimal guidance from me as a coach. All that I did was to ensure that they had sound basics, and then I let them express themselves naturally. In my own case, I never had any lessons myself and yet managed to win numerous titles above club level as an adult, having only taken the game up as a serious hobby when I was twenty-five – all based on my own ability and determination. Frankly, it is my honest opinion that any coaching I might have had would have simply held me back. You will appreciate this sad aspect of British tennis more and more as you plough your way through this chapter.

There now follow many examples that support the basic tenet of this chapter: i.e. that coaches in Great Britain are not trained properly. I have included so many – and there are even more that I have left out – because I want to convince you, the reader, that the problem is, indeed, serious, and affects, and will continue to affect, any chance that an aspiring junior in the UK has of ever becoming world-class.

Once again, there has to be a HEALTH WARNING:

Please read on, but do not feel guilty about leaving the chapter once you have got the gist, the health and balance of your mental state are important to me. With the invaluable help, once more, of my co-author, I try to add humour and a light touch wherever possible, so that the sheer gravity of the mess does not weigh too heavily on you and detract from the pleasure that one should derive from reading. I know I have said this before, but I think it is worth repeating. Be warned, though, if you do decide to skip some sections, you may miss out on some veritable gems. But, above all, please take it easy.

And if you are a coach, please do not despair: what you are about to read is simply the result of poor training. I too was once in the same thoroughly unsatisfactory position myself.

First, a quote from the 2006 Blueprint: 'In the community we will ensure that we have enough of the right coaches working in our schools and parks – coaches who have the talent to get players of all ages up, rallying and enjoying the game, fast! They will become the pied pipers of tennis'.

It is my considered opinion that this constant cry from LTA tutors to 'get players rallying and enjoying the game fast' is the very reason our juniors seldom develop sound basics. In fact, it reveals a flawed approach to the business of teaching tennis.

You have to learn to play the strokes correctly in the initial stages before rallying, and certainly before playing matches. In between lessons, juniors can of course have a go with their friends and even enter a few competitions if they really want to, but this plays no part in proper learning. You may consider my approach to be very different to that of other coaches, and even to be boring.

But quite the opposite is true: every Easter I was fully booked until December year after year, and the only time I really needed to advertise for customers was for my summer holiday courses, never for my week-to-week programmes. This is why I stayed in coaching when I had more than enough reasons to get out, if you can still remember the horrors from the last chapter.

However, coaches who concentrate on getting their juniors 'rallying and enjoying the game fast' may make it fun and appear to be successful, but it does not last, and the juniors soon leave because they realise they are not making much progress, and actually get bored with the 'fun' approach. On the other hand, the youngsters following my programmes have consistently stayed much longer – years longer, in fact – than they do with most other coaches, because they are aware that they are learning in a structured and logical way, and it all makes sense to them.

Let the examples begin.

While I was sitting beside some school tennis courts waiting for my pupils to arrive, I remember watching a top-qualified coach teaching the serve to a class of girls. I observed with interest as all eight girls tossed their ball up to serve in the same wrong place, and the coach quite correctly recognised this. 'No, girls, throw the ball in front, not to the right – you are all making the same mistake,' he informed them.

After spending five minutes successfully practising the ball toss in isolation, with racquets placed on the ground, the entire class returned again to serving. But, with no surprise to me, they all started throwing the ball to their right once more, and serving with completely the wrong technique. The problem was not the girls' inability to throw the ball in the correct place, because all eight girls had proved they could throw the ball in the correct serving position during their five minutes of practice, when not holding their racquets. The problem was the tennis coach: he had not properly identified what caused them to throw the ball too far to the right each time. Bear in mind, all eight girls were suffering from the same problem, which, I might add, was, and is, easy to cure.

What a complete waste of a serving lesson, and from, on paper at least, a highly-qualified tennis coach! There is only one reason the coach was not able to help those eight girls – he had not learnt his trade properly. As I have already stated, after my first LTA qualification course I would have fared no better.

It pains me to say that this is typical of British coaching, and not only at grass-roots level, and results in players either giving up in frustration, as they continually fail, like the eight girls in this example, or, at the very least, making little progress because of incorrect coaching. With a coach like this for guidance, what hope does an aspiring junior, or any junior, for that matter, have of fulfilling his potential?

The incredible thing about this particular example of poor coaching is that I happen to be referring to the most important stroke in the game, as you may well know, with the most common fault that a coach will come across when teaching it – and it is not the ball toss. Moreover, the solution to the problem also involves the most important technical aspect of the serve. And yet, out of at least fifty coaches I have spoken to about this frequently occurring phenomenon, not one knew the correct way to rectify it.

Such a situation strikes me as appalling. If a highly-qualified coach, or any coach for that matter, cannot offer the correct diagnosis for the biggest technical problem in parks and club tennis, i.e. the grass roots and just above, how on earth can we help our youngsters make progress and stand a chance of reaching the higher echelons of the game? Why were these coaches allowed to qualify?

In my opinion, coaches simply have to understand the technical basics of tennis and how to teach them. It is all very well a coach being good at teaching tactics, or having umpteen drills and team games ready for when coaching large groups to make lessons fun, but, the majority of the time, drills, team games and tactics are not ultimately what a player needs.

Some coaches explain to me that they are fitness gurus, or they specialise in doubles play, or concentrate mainly on the sports psychology side of the game when coaching. Well, that is fine, and I applaud and respect these coaches who I am sure teach these aspects of tennis very well, but they must have a thorough understanding of the basics on the technical side as well, if they want to call themselves tennis coaches.

Players need technical adjustments over 80% of the time in the early years, so you simply cannot call yourself a good coach if you step on to the court without the knowledge of how to make these necessary adjustments. What is the point of drilling a player on his backhand side, if the backhand he is playing is woefully lacking technically, or trying to improve the stroke by giving him more belief and confidence? It is completely the wrong way to go about things.

For the eight girls trying to learn how to serve, and paying good money for a professional tennis lesson, the chances of any of them becoming competent players are virtually nil. I should mention that, ironically, the serving lesson was quite likely to trigger off tennis elbow, just to add to their problems. So this would have made them give up for a time anyway. And some of them might never have returned to tennis because of such a negative experience, having come to the conclusion that, as a sport, it is almost impossible to play properly – you cannot even make headway with the stroke that starts off every game, and, into the bargain, when you try, under the guidance of a fully-qualified coach, you end up with a very painful injury.

It also has to be recognised that, since the sport is so technical, the first time you walk on to a tennis court virtually determines the sort of player you will become: with good coaching, the possibilities are endless; with bad coaching, it is not even worth talking about possibilities.

Let us resume this tale of woe.

Quite by chance, while having a casual hit with my daughter, I once witnessed alongside me an entire lesson when a coach threw easy balls for a ten year-old girl to hit with her forehand drive. The balls went everywhere and anywhere, completely out of control, because the girl's technique was terrible, and it was obvious she did not know what she should be doing. Without one word of corrective advice, but with much encouragement to keep trying, the coach eventually gave up and resorted to fun games of catch and tennis hockey, and suchlike, for forty minutes.

In the last ten minutes the coach returned to the first

drill of hitting forehand drives. More comments of 'bad luck' and 'nearly', and 'well done', if by chance the ball did occasionally land in, but, without any proper technical instruction, the poor ten year-old was no better off at playing tennis than at the start.

Her mother then paid an individual coaching fee, thanked the coach, and off the two went, confirming the daughter would be back for more so-called coaching the following week. What a waste of time and money. What a disgrace for the LTA Coaching Department, who passed this coach as qualified, but did not teach him what constitutes a technically sound forehand drive. And following on from the earlier poor coaching of the serve – the most important stroke in the game – we now have the poor coaching of the forehand drive – the second most important stroke in the game.

Another example of inept coaching I happened to come across involved the repetition of the words 'head up' to a junior hoping to learn to serve, when there were at least four classic technical serving faults which had nothing to do with one's head being up, down or sideways. This was followed by the coach repeating the word 'punch' as the junior attempted, in vain, to play a backhand volley, again with the most common technical faults, which desperately needed attention before any punching could be considered.

Yet another case, then, of £30 or more being wasted by a parent believing he is paying for the best tuition available. And this happened at a top tennis club from a top coach while I was watching a junior tournament, so, in theory, the junior could not have received better teaching in the whole of the UK. I personally would not be happy with this level of coaching even if it were from a PE teacher trying to offer his pupil a little help, let alone a full-time professional tennis coach.

The trouble is, when players make little progress, they put it down to their own lack of ability rather than attach any blame to the coach, who, of course, holds those wonderful qualifications and has managed to play to such a high standard himself. So how can a charming, polite, humorous, and most encouraging and enthusiastic qualified tennis coach be to blame? And, if the coach is working at a large tennis club, then he must be very good at his job. On top of this, the parent thinks that they can actually see some improvement in their ten year-old, so naturally attribute this to the tuition received from the coach. But I am afraid this is not the reason for the pupil's apparent progress.

Anyone who has taken up tennis for the first time and played once a week for six months or more without lessons will improve, and therefore will appear to be making progress. But all that really happens is that the individual becomes more familiar with the racquet, gets used to judging the ball and moving to it, and learns his own way to swing the racquet and control the ball far better than the very first time he stepped on to the court. Progress of a kind you could say, but very limited, and most certainly not sound development.

But, unless this individual is super-talented, has observed top players in action, and has the ability to imitate incredibly well, the apparent progress is usually very false indeed. To play a stroke with consistency, accuracy, control, power and spin requires a sound technique. And the rare individual who appears to achieve this using his own technique will invariably tell me it all seems to go haywire under pressure, or when he attempts to hit the ball with more pace. So, as I say, and always will until my dying day, technique is everything.

How do you think those Ryder Cup golfers manage to tee off on the first hole when they admit afterwards how much they were shaking over the ball, contemplating that one shot? The answer, of course, is that their technique is so good – they know that they can trust it, and it gets them through such tense moments, even when mentally they are in bits.

So the truth is: a lot of tennis coaches in this country cannot coach properly. And whose fault is it? It has to be down to those who train them: they do it incorrectly, and then hand out the qualification certificates. And off the newly-qualified coaches go, into sports centres, schools, parks and tennis clubs, without any real clue as to how to coach properly, and, what is more, most of them are just not aware of their own shortcomings. Why should they be? They have never experienced, or been shown how to deliver, a proper coaching lesson, so they think they are doing well.

As juniors, they attended poor coaching; then they are trained in the same way by their tutors, hearing the same jargon, which reinforces for them that this is the way to coach. The qualification certificate that follows simply rubber-stamps their fitness and right to teach tennis, so off they go, armed with fine phrases of encouragement for their pupils, but in no way ready to coach in the true sense of the word. As I have already said, it is not the coaches' fault, but a vicious circle has been created, and nobody has realised it, or, if anyone has, they have certainly not dared to speak out about it – until now.

Unlike schoolteachers, who periodically face an Ofsted inspection, the coach is accountable to nobody. It is all too easy for him, especially in the sense that he can get away with bad coaching, and there is no comeback whatsoever. And, just to make matters worse, it is all too easy to obtain a coaching qualification as well. Moreover, if, as a player, the coach played for his county, or attained a rating of 5 or better, the qualification is virtually handed to him before the course commences. No wonder British tennis is in such a mess. But please do not despair: there is a solution on its way, and it is in this book. In the meantime, however, I am compelled to carry on with the theme of this chapter, as depressing as it is, because it concerns a reality that needs to be fully understood and appreciated in all its appalling magnitude.

Even our best juniors suffer from too many technically bad and ingrained habits which they were allowed to acquire through the poor coaching given to them when they first started. The more talented players do appear to get round unsatisfactory coaching to a certain degree, and manage to make their strokes work, but I am afraid that, at the very top level, they get found out.

This, in essence, is why we fail to produce players who are capable of getting into the world's top 100. It is the number one reason, far outweighing any other improvements that we might think are necessary. Nowadays, the standard is so high at the top of the sport that you cannot afford to have little flaws in any part of your game. Each stroke must be set fundamentally in place from early on in your development, otherwise, as I have already said, under pressure, a player cannot rely on controlling the ball with the speed, spin and accuracy that are essential at the very highest level.

Talented players will have days when their strokes seem to be flowing, but they know themselves how, for no apparent reason, their serve, or backhand drive, for example, suddenly deserts them, and just when they need it most. I have just said 'for no apparent reason', but there IS most certainly a reason: it is all down to tiny but significant flaws in their technique.

Ask Sue Barker about her backhand drive. I can hear her saying: 'Oh, don't, I'm trying to forget it – it was awful'. And yet here was someone with great talent who played brilliantly to win the French Open, despite carrying such a handicap in her game. I am sure that some people will not like what I have just written: how dare I criticise such an outstanding British tennis player who won eleven titles in singles and twelve in doubles during her career? After all, we are not exactly over-endowed with success in world tennis, as we all know. Unfortunately, what I am referring to is reality, which is what this book is about.

Coming nearer to the present time, may I remind you that Tim Henman has criticised British coaching for not sorting his serve out better when still a teenager. He is on record as saying that he felt he never really got the advice he was looking for. As has been said in the book already, with a more powerful serve, Tim would almost certainly have won Wimbledon – he was, in fact, only a couple of serves away from doing so.

And to bring us right up to date, Andy Murray has said about his brother: 'Jamie was more talented than me, but chose to stay with the LTA coaching system for his development, while I opted to train in Spain'. It is worth remembering that, at under-12 level, Jamie had been ranked number 2 in the world in singles, but, after his spell with the LTA in Cambridge, his game fell apart and never recovered, according to his mother, Judy, leading him eventually to specialise in doubles only. And the less talented brother won Wimbledon! Does that not say it all?

And on the same subject, I am reminded of a very good question that was asked in a Radio 5 programme by a tennis enthusiast during the Wimbledon Championships of 2005. There was a very young Andy Murray, getting all the attention and playing brilliantly, and, if it had not been for his relative lack of fitness at the time, Andy might easily have beaten the Wimbledon finalist of 2002, David Nalbandian of Argentina, in the third round.

'Is it not true,' the questioner asked, 'that Andy Murray has learnt to play tennis in Spain, not Britain?' Whereupon, an LTA representative confidently replied that it was true that Andy had developed there for over two years, but one had to realise that it was Britain which had developed him from the age of ten to fourteen, and this had a lot to do with his success.

My point here would simply be: if the LTA had been so good at developing Andy Murray for four years, then what happened to the thousands of other girls and boys who were presumably being coached just as well as Andy over those same four years, or even longer if they had started with an LTA coach at the age of five or six? In other words, why is it, out of, say, 10,000 youngsters up and down the country, the one player who opted to complete his development outside the British system makes it to the very top of world tennis, while the other 9,999 all fall by the wayside? Why did not half a dozen, at the very least, make it into the world's top 100 like Andy, if the coaching for our ten to fourteen year-olds was up to scratch? This is, of course, a rhetorical question.

These are the facts, but will anyone take note and make real changes to our coaching system?

You may be interested to know that I have tried to explain my ideas to the LTA. The first time was in 1996, when I had proven to my own satisfaction how little technical expertise so many British coaches possessed. I presented a significant technical aspect I had worked out to two people at the top of the Coaching Department – an aspect, incidentally, that I had already incorporated very successfully into my own coaching system. I only presented it after being badgered by several other coaches who urged me to share my methods with the LTA.

But my technical ideas were dismissed out of hand, and even laughed at, with absolutely no proper consideration of what I had discovered, despite the fact that I showed them pictures of the top players doing exactly what I was explaining to them. 'We know best', of course.

However, I did get some belated and welcome recognition of a sort when, in the September 2001 *Ace* magazine, a team of coaching experts from America announced that they had just discovered the same technical point I had presented to the LTA five years earlier. I still have the dismissive letter from the LTA, my coaching example, and the *Ace* magazine for anyone to see, that is, if they are interested. Of course, if it had been Tim Henman presenting the same idea, then I am sure it would have been taken much more seriously. As has been stated before, fame is a wonderful seductive agent.

Perhaps I should have complained to the LTA Coaching Department after I first qualified in 1985 on their 'Elementary' course, as it was then known, especially since I was the only candidate to be passed with 'distinction' – they just might have been prepared to listen to what I had to say. It would not, though, have been very pleasant to hear: I would have told them that I felt quite incapable of teaching a single tennis stroke to anyone.

To explain further, as far as the actual teaching of tennis was concerned – the different techniques needed, how to combine the strokes, learning about basic tactics, and the difference between singles and doubles – there was absolutely nothing offered in the course on such vital matters.

In wishing to become a competent tennis coach, as I said in Chapter 1, I simply knew I had to get away from the LTA system, because, having qualified with distinction and been encouraged to get out there and teach talented juniors, and others as well, I knew myself that I did not know where to start, and could not have coached even a beginner stepping on to a tennis court for the first time.

And the incredible thing is, I can say this having attended an LTA qualification course delivered by someone considered to be one of the best tutors in the UK. While I appreciate that it all took place a long time ago, in discussing the content of LTA courses since then with coaches who have been on them, I can assure you that there is still no method or system in existence, and lectures have just been wrapped and presented in different clothing as the LTA continually revamp – sorry, 'update' – the qualification structure.

Newly-qualified coaches I have talked to simply do not know the basics of the techniques used in tennis strokes – that is the stark and sad reality of it all, and this is in spite of all the impressive-looking literature produced by the LTA on how to train players from the age of six to twenty-plus, and, we must not forget, the dazzling plethora of courses, and extra accreditation courses, on offer. What coaches do have in abundance, however, are drills and tennis-related games, coupled usually with humorous asides and words of encouragement, on which lesson after lesson is based.

If a player asks his coach for help with his backhand topspin passing shot because he considers it is letting him down in matches, the coach is likely to set up a drill which incorporates this shot. But all that this does is highlight the problem the player is having. There is no analysis of the shot, or any real change introduced, in order to bring about any improvement. In effect, the coach is providing practice for the player, not correction. 'Practice makes permanent' – so again we are creating ingrained habits which a player may never recover from.

Any aspiring junior receiving such coaching is doomed to mediocrity at the very best, unless he quickly changes to a proper coach, if there is one nearby. Even without the fault being a technical one, drills are not the answer to everyone's problems, and yet too often, as this next example indicates, this is all a typical British coach can usually offer.

Having given the ladies' teams of a club coaching on doubles play, the coach who replaced me the following season was asked to provide the same. But, instead of explaining the correct positions and finer tactics of doubles play as I had done, the new coach merely set up doubles drills, without any real coaching on any of the following: who should chase the lob; or when to approach the net; or volley down the line; or intercept. And, despite a second request for positional and tactical coaching from the ladies' captain, the coach just continued with drills, and encouragement, or 'white noise', with the odd joke thrown in, which, as the captain wryly commented, she herself could have dreamt up. 'That wasn't coaching', I recall her telling me, and she was right, but, of course, by then she had had the experience of what proper doubles coaching should be like.

The drills just made the ladies play the same way as they had always done – there was no learning or improvement. It is interesting how so many coaches think that they are giving such good lessons by constantly using drills, when, in truth, they are merely cementing a player's problems further.

Quite frankly, as I stated in Chapter 5, the coaching system in the UK is crying out for a complete and radical rethink, and that is putting it mildly, although I should add that my solution, which comes later, would not be that difficult to implement, nor would it cost loads of money for the LTA to set up or for coaches to attend.

It is worth repeating that many excuses have been offered by the governing body of British tennis for their inability to produce top players. Once they had given up with the 'we just need one top player' excuse, since Tim Henman disproved that theory, having been around for a number of years, and still the rest of the Brits failed to make it into the top 100, they came up with the following: 'We are fine at producing players up to the age of fifteen, but our coaches cannot develop them into world-class players'.

I lost count of the number of top people in British tennis who cottoned on to this statement as the reason for Britain not producing world-beaters, and went around referring to it as being the only problem we had to overcome. It sounded good, so, with no other obvious excuse to recite, everyone jumped on the bandwagon. I must have read it, or heard it repeated, fifty times over. At least, it was an admission that British tennis had a coaching problem, even if only admitting to it at the advanced and final stage of a junior's development.

A move in the right direction, certainly, and at last getting away from the old excuses of poor climate, insufficient indoor courts, and suchlike. But, in my opinion, the LTA were again barking up the wrong tree, all because they simply did not, and do not, know the reality of tennis in the UK. In actual fact, the problem lies at the very bottom, at grass-roots level, when players are just starting out.

I recall a comment made by Carl Maes, the famous Belgian employed by the LTA, referred to in Chapter 5, who had been coach to none other than Justine Henin-Hardenne and Kim Clijsters, simultaneously numbers 1 and 2 in the world at one time.

Carl said that he was very disappointed with the standard of our best twelve to fifteen year-olds, stating that they were well behind the rest of the world at this age. And he was right. The only conclusion one can come to from his judgement is that Britain's fifteen year-olds were not as good as the LTA were claiming. The real problem is that the technical ability of our best fifteen year-olds is so poor that coaches are having to try and develop them using their insecure fundamentals. But, no matter how much effort and energy coaches put in, it just does not work.

Weak basics in tennis do not go away. You have to remould completely – that is, if it is not too late, and, most importantly, if the junior concerned actually recognises that he needs to make changes, and is willing to do so. It is like constructing a building: if the foundations are substandard, then decorate it well both inside and out, and all will appear to be fine, but, under pressure, and in a short space of time, such a building will crumble to the ground. The foundations have to be solid to stand up in all weathers and over the long term.

Tennis strokes are the same, and, like buildings where the only solution would be to knock them down and start again to give a solid foundation, so a player's basic technique must be remodelled before he can move on with any success. But it is too late for our sixteen to nineteen year-olds, if they have not already developed sound basics. Their chance has gone, as they are generally too set in their ways by this time, and are likely to be reluctant to change anyway, since they most probably have experienced some success thus far.

The reason we may compete well around the world at fifteen and under, as the LTA have noticed and results have proved, is that, while our technique is inadequate, the other three factors in becoming world-class are also still in their development stage, and will be for all fifteen year-olds, whatever their nationality. Our mental, tactical and physical ability to play tennis will match, if not better, those from around the world, so, at this early stage, we can compete with the best, as the foreign youngsters are still developing in all four areas of tennis as well. By the time the overseas juniors have reached twenty, however, all four areas of their tennis development are complete, including their technique, so they become the next generation ranked in the top 100.

For the Brits, three of the four requirements are in place, certainly, but their basic fundamentals were not taught correctly, so their technique is simply not solid enough, and cannot be put right. They are therefore doomed to mediocrity and failure. This is the simple but sad reality of the situation.

Occasionally, of course, you will get the odd early developer who comes through between the ages of fourteen and seventeen, showing precociously good development in all four areas required to become world-class. If we are just as good as the rest of the world up to the age of fifteen, as the LTA claim, then how come we never produce a successful world-class player in the senior game well before they have reached their eighteenth birthday?

Such youngsters come from everywhere but Britain. Players like Dokic, Lucic, Capriati, Hingis, Krickstein,

Chang, Becker, Arantxa Sánchez Vicario, Austin, Jaeger, Nadal, Gasquet. The list is most impressive, and there are many more, but funny how you cannot name any young players who were coached in Britain. All these young greats of tennis could compete with the world's top 10 at sixteen years of age.

These are the facts – reality again – as ugly and unthinkable as they may sound to the LTA and even to you, the reader. So it is not our inability to develop sixteen and seventeen year-olds into world-class players over their next three to four years, but our inability to prepare them properly right from the very first time they pick up a racquet.

One of the reasons for our juniors not being able to develop sound technical basics was brought home to me when I was invited to take two talented brothers, of around twelve years of age, to join a top county under-14 squad for an indoor session. The coach, impressively a player with a world ranking at the time, took the eight junior boys for two hours.

After twenty minutes of agility work and fitness runs, they were asked to count the number of errors in a service box rallying drill. Then they had to recall the number of successfully hit consecutive shots when rallying from the baseline, followed by some serving practice, with the emphasis on placement, then power. The session finished up with some singles games.

Before leaving, I questioned the boy struggling the most with his backhand, as he could only poke at the ball – that is, if he did not manage to run round it and hit it with his powerful forehand topspin – and he confirmed that the three sessions each week were always like this, adding that he did not attend any other coaching and that he was desperate to improve his backhand.

What appals me is that any schoolteacher could deliver a tennis lesson like this. What tennis or coaching knowledge do you need? It is absolutely typical of what happens in Britain, with not a word of technical instruction uttered to anyone, when this was so obviously necessary. I cannot begin to tell you how frustrating it was to watch talented boys playing so erratically and out of control, particularly on their backhand side, where they all had problems of one sort or another, and also to see them with serves which desperately needed technical adjustments, and this shot, as we know, is the most important in the game.

Any potential they ever had of developing into top players was rapidly disappearing with each hapless session. Such juniors, and others like them, would be the very players the Belgian, Carl Maes, was aiming his comments at. It should be pointed out that, by the time such youngsters reach the age of sixteen, they have become stronger, quicker, wiser, tactically better, and have learnt to cope with the inadequacies of their strokes.

But asking them to change their technique to allow them to perform on the international stage with any success is not realistic. For these aspiring juniors, dreaming of a successful tennis-playing career, it is a tragedy: it is not their fault at all that they have no chance of making it, and the whole sorry saga could have been avoided with proper coaching in their very early, formative years.

In the post '2006 Blueprint' era, county training no longer exists: instead, we now have Performance Centres all over the country – seventy-two in number from 2012 to 2017 – at specially designated clubs, where children as young as five or six, or even younger tots, can learn how to play by following mini tennis courses and using low compression balls that are easy to control. Later on, when they are older and progress to normal yellow balls, those with the most talent and promise can move on to one of the seventeen High Performance Centres for more advanced and intensive training.

Children can also learn at any club, big or small, that offers mini tennis, as well as on some park courts in 'Tennis in the Park' schemes run by the LTA, and also by Tennis For Free (TFF), set up by Tony Hawks.

It all seems very impressive, but, inevitably, the progress that the children make depends entirely on the coaches. Despite the special LTA mini tennis courses the coaches should have been on, and visits to the Performance Centres from the county Talent and Performance Coordinator, the situation is still the same as it was a few years ago, with technically deficient training producing technically deficient coaching. To put it simply and starkly, all those involved in teaching mini tennis, wherever they operate, should be knowledgeable enough to get the youngsters started in the right way, from the absolutely crucial viewpoint of technique. They should know at all times what to look for and how to correct it.

In 2013, while waiting for a friend to come out of the changing rooms, I was able to observe a mini tennis group lesson for seven to nine year-olds at a prestigious indoor centre, which was also an official LTA Performance Centre. There were three coaches, so the children had the chance to rally over a mini tennis net with a coach on their own. One eight year-old girl appeared particularly athletic and enthusiastic, and eventually completed a four-stroke rally. 'Fantastic,' shouted the coach and immediately stepped up to the net in order to give the girl a high five. And high fives were all I kept seeing, which the children responded to with great enthusiasm. One coach's vocabulary seemed to be limited to just four words over a forty-five minute period: 'Fantastic', 'yes', and 'come on'.

The aforementioned eight year-old played forehands sometimes with one hand, sometimes with two hands, and sometimes with two hands the other way round on the racquet. She also played shots single-handedly as both a left- and right-handed player, and it was obvious she had become quite familiar with playing in so many different ways. She could not have been in a worse mess with her tennis if she had tried, and was having great difficulty in controlling the ball. It was pure chance and racquet familiarity which enabled her occasionally to complete a rally of four shots, and, of course, this rewarded her with another high five. Not one of the three coaches, all of whom were supervising her, ever corrected this girl in any way at all, let alone sort out her chronic grip problem.

The reality of what has just been described is in complete contrast to what the LTA 'Talent Identification' website for this age group states: 'Tennis is a very technical sport', and 'If a young player is showing strong signs of physical, technical and tactical development their coach will have the opportunity to nominate them for a County Talent ID Day'. No chance, then, of any of these juniors showing any signs of technical or tactical development, let alone 'strong' signs. And this was a Performance Centre!

I would have liked to intervene on behalf of the eight year-old, but, who am I? Just a humble and simple grass-roots coach. It is also interesting that, in the written LTA Training Programme for mini tennis, the different grips are never mentioned, but I am sure that such an important aspect of learning tennis is referred to in some detail on mini tennis courses, it has to be, or am I being too optimistic here? The fact is, of course – the coaches were not doing their jobs properly.

However, the coaches might argue in their defence that they were doing exactly what they had been directed to do on their courses: make it fun; get them hitting lots of balls; do some rallying; and keep them running around. Full marks, then. But when will the juniors actually be taught anything?

The children were enjoying the lesson, certainly, but they were so woefully lacking in guidance that one wonders how on earth they were going to make progress towards acquiring anything like the technical proficiency that would enable them to sustain a controlled rally of any length. As far as Trade Descriptions go, this Performance Centre was falling way short of what it was purporting to be.

You have to ask whether this completely haphazard and unstructured approach would ever happen in any other kind of lesson, be it in sport, or any other activity, given by a fully-qualified professional. As stated already, an LTA Training Programme certainly exists for mini tennis, but it needs well-prepared coaches who fully understand it, and are conscientious enough to implement it properly. Does having fun override everything else, including how to hold the racquet properly? What I witnessed in this Performance Centre was equivalent to a child having a piano lesson and just being allowed to smash the white and black keys with fist and fingers at random, creating a veritable cacophony of sound, with the teacher not offering any constructive or corrective advice. Of course, this would be unthinkable, and no piano teacher would ever conduct a lesson in this way, but it happens in tennis!

As we have already seen, parents pay the money in good

faith, and, in this case, expect the Performance Centre to perform – i.e. to teach their children how to play properly. The parents see that most of the coaches are of a very good playing standard – county, or at least a rating of 5 – and naturally think that they will do a good job with their children, hopefully getting them to a similar level, if not higher. Most will know little about coaching systems and qualifications, so will assume everything is fine, even if it does occur to a few that there is an excess of fun, and not much hard learning going on. As long as no one complains, and the courses are filled, everyone is happy, including the county Talent and Performance Coordinator, it seems.

Well, I have to say in no uncertain terms that I, for one, am most definitely not happy, and I hope that, as a result of what I write, many will see that I am justified in questioning it all most seriously.

'Well-organised shapes', i.e. for each stroke, are impressively mentioned in the LTA Training Programme for players aged six to twenty-plus, and, yet, some coaches, not coaching assistants but fully-qualified coaches, teaching mini tennis, even in Performance Centres, do not have such shapes themselves in their own game, so how can they be sure of teaching the different shots properly? And do such coaches appreciate and understand the nuts and bolts of it all?

I have yet to come across a coach who can explain clearly and in detail the shape for each stroke in tennis, let alone teach it to an absolute beginner. Can such coaches really see the specific problem a child may be having with a particular shot and put it right immediately, which is what should happen, rather than allow it to drag on lesson after lesson?

Then there is the constant tug-of-war between FUN and

actual teaching: the catchphrase for mini tennis is 'Play and stay' – in other words, make it fun, or else the youngsters will give up. Of course, a good teacher, or coach, should get the balance right between fun and learning, organising appropriate activities for the age of the pupils in the class. And, in any case, fun and learning need not be mutually exclusive: in my opinion, you can teach properly from the start and incorporate a suitable amount of fun as part of the learning process. In this way, the pupils will not only have fun, but will also experience something much more lasting called satisfaction – i.e. the satisfaction derived from learning tennis properly.

If a five or six year-old, for example, can start to hit a forehand drive that is both consistent and stylish, i.e. technically correct, soon after taking up mini tennis, because he has been coached properly from the very start, is that not the progress that will delight the parents who are paying, and will it not, in turn, motivate the youngster to carry on learning? ('I'm getting good at this'). It is well worth reiterating here that successful professional players often started hitting a ball, with technical guidance, well before the age of five.

During the 2013 US Open Judy Murray said on Sky Sports that eleven to twelve year-olds should already be able to play with variety, showing an appreciation and understanding of the different spins in tennis – in other words, they must be aware that it is not all about hitting the ball hard for a quick winner, but, rather, about constructing a point in order to find an opening. How can a youngster reach such a level if he is not taught the different techniques properly and thoroughly for the many different strokes that exist in tennis? There are, in fact, more than twenty of them.

As I have said before, the learning process can, and should, start in the very first lesson. There is such a lot to learn and time is short: too much fun, in isolation, is nothing more than a distraction and a hindrance. Performance Centres should be about performance and progress – only then will they become 'hives of talent development', as the 2006 Blueprint has it. This, though, will only happen if the coaches know how to perform as well. The same, of course, goes for the mini tennis that is taught elsewhere – in clubs and parks.

Some youngsters are so relieved and happy when they come to me for coaching because they immediately realise that I am all about teaching them how to get the ball over the net with a sound technique, in complete contrast to the FUN approach they have experienced elsewhere. It is significant that a coach in charge of a mini tennis programme at a Performance Centre confided to my co-author that some youngsters do not develop the 'shapes' of the LTA Training Programme as quickly, or as well, as they should.

Quite frankly, such a state of affairs is down to a lack of quality in the coaching, and a lack of emphasis on technical teaching.

If you, the reader, ever have the opportunity to observe some coaching for a while, you will soon realise that 90% of the time the emphasis is on fun and a variety of little team and individual games, with much running around. In my opinion, a good group session may well start with five minutes of running about as a warm-up – and a very useful ploy to allow latecomers to arrive – before the proper coaching starts. It can then end with ten minutes of team games and fun, certainly, but the middle forty-five minutes must be made up of the technical teaching of the strokes in a non-pressured situation, so that the players really develop their tennis correctly. This is progress – something I definitely put ahead of fun in my lessons. It is nothing more than common sense to structure classes in this way. It is also good teaching – something that parents and their children not only prefer, but also appreciate and respond to. Why else would they come for tennis lessons?

It is all too easy for a coach just to organise 'fun' games for children week after week as a lazy way out, rather than do the hard graft of coaching properly.

It is not surprising at all that parents sometimes move their children from one Performance Centre to another in the same area, or county, in search of what they perceive to be better coaching, or a better regime. And, if a coach who was once ranked in the top 200 or 300 starts working at a Centre, there is almost a stampede for his services – such is the desperation of the more serious-minded parents for the best possible guidance for their children.

It also, perhaps, shows the dissatisfaction that exists with the mini tennis set-up and the philosophy that underpins it – if you want them to 'stay and play', make it fun! In the past, selecting the best juniors in a county for special training was an idea that should have worked, and perhaps did work in a few cases, but, at present, in the same Performance Centre, there can be a real mixture of talent and seriousness, or lack of it, creating an atmosphere that is frankly not conducive to performance. Moreover, it is not very inspiring to enrol at a Performance Centre that cannot attract enough children on to its mini tennis programmes, even after Wimbledon, 2013. Who can blame parents for looking elsewhere? In one large and well-known commercial indoor centre some of the coaches taking mini tennis did not even know that they were working at an official LTA Performance Centre until my co-author informed them!

Then we have the High Performance Centres for promising

players as they get older and better. Some will have LTA funding to help pay for their training, having achieved some success in regional and national competitions. Unfortunately, what happens at these Centres is very similar to what happened to my two twelve year-old boys who joined the county under-14 squad for a training session: first of all, it is fitness and agility work, then drills, and, finally, some competitive games, but no, or very little, technical teaching, even when it is patently obvious that a number of the players desperately need it in different areas. As has been said before, the philosophy is: keep trying to get it right, hit lots of balls and, in the end, you will get it right. As a coach, I can tell you quite categorically that such an approach simply does not work. Just observe a fifty year-old experienced player of recreational standard with unorthodox strokes, and you will discover that he has not improved in the last twenty years, despite playing two or three times a week.

To stop you reaching for the Prozac, I should remind you that there is a chapter called 'The Solution' later on in the book – it is always good to have something to look forward to. And, while on the subject of Prozac, I do wonder sometimes if there are coaches in the UK who have to resort to such medication because they find themselves in virtual limbo – in a void, even – with no real syllabus to follow, no real system, and no real method, and, to boot, no union to take up their case.

In 2013 a number of coaches complained to the LTA that their particular website rarely contained anything of relevance, and, on top of that, it was 'too complicated'. The simple truth is that coaches need proper support, proper guidance, and proper training: if all this were in place, the mess would not exist, and I would never have put pen to paper – what a relief that would have been!

Reality dictates that we cannot pretend the problem is anything but serious. As mentioned before, a few more courts here, a bit of money thrown there or, more accurately, lots of money, more tennis in schools and parks, and schemes to get more juniors playing tennis are not going to make any difference at all. We have tried all that for decades.

In fashion at the time of writing is the numbers game — there is even a new catchphrase at the LTA: 'Tennis, a game for everyone'. This has now changed to: 'Getting more people playing tennis, more often'. The thinking is, if you get more people playing, even if it is only Cardio tennis, the knock-on effect will be simply amazing, with untold talent being unearthed and champions eventually emerging. And, of course, with increased participation, Sport England might well be persuaded to release the millions that were withheld in December, 2012, and Baroness Billingham could even decide to refrain from calling the LTA 'useless'.

However, as with many things in British tennis, the argument about numbers is flawed. Let me compare this strategy to that of Grand Prix motor racing. If our mechanics did not have the expertise to fine-tune the engine to a world-class level, it would result in our British cars always trailing in last in Grands Prix, so hand these same mechanics more cars, and the result will simply be more cars trailing in last. How can it result in any other way? The mechanics in tennis are the coaches, of course, constructing and fine-tuning juniors' tennis strokes. Fail to fine-tune our juniors perfectly, i.e. not teach them perfect technique, and they will come last in the top tournaments. So, if we double the number of juniors being coached, then we only double the number of juniors failing to break into the world's top

100, or getting anywhere near it. A harsh statement, you may think, but, if you believe what I am telling you, then you will become acutely and painfully aware that this is nothing more than the reality of British tennis.

You may find it difficult to accept, but allow me to remind you that I am also a coach who once passed his first LTA qualification course, and was hopeless at coaching, as I have already indicated in this chapter and an earlier one. I joined the vast majority of coaches in this country who have frankly never coached well enough to put Britain on the world tennis map, and that is being euphemistic. But it was not our fault. After all, the coaches were, and still are, only coaching according to the training given by the LTA. I fully recognise that I was in exactly the same boat once, but having qualified, I at least realised I had deficiencies and did something about them before I coached full-time.

What may interest you is why it occurred to me in the first place that I could not coach, when I was the county number 2, a county champion, and was often competing against full-time players, while the other coaches accepted what was taught on their qualification courses, and went out and taught what they had learnt, believing they were coaching to a perfectly adequate or even good, standard.

I did not accept the training from the LTA because, at the time I attended the course, I had never had a tennis lesson in my life. Unlike many other trainee coaches, this gave me the distinct advantage of not having any preconceived ideas about tennis coaching. On top of this, I was already a qualified table tennis coach, having attended a lengthy qualification course, with logical steps for teaching someone to play properly from beginner to advanced, and with real ways to overcome difficulties often encountered by the less talented player. Everything had made sense, and I could relate it all to my own table tennis game and techniques that I used.

You cannot imagine how shocked I was by the content of the new, improved LTA Elementary coaches' course I followed and passed. I did voice my concerns at the end, but was frowned upon, so I immediately looked elsewhere to learn my trade, which fortunately turned out to be my breakthrough in tennis coaching. Perhaps I should be grateful for the LTA coaching system being sufficiently poor to make me search elsewhere for my training. As I wrote in Chapter 1, I would certainly like to thank the Kenyan, Piers Bastard, from whom I learnt the basics of tennis coaching.

It has to be said that most coaches accept the jargon and catchphrases used on their courses because they are a repeat of how they were coached for years as juniors, so now, third time round, they are bound to coach along the same lines, making a few adjustments as they see fit, and as suits their style.

Furthermore, unlike what happens in schoolteaching, there are no inspectors to check up on coaches either, so nobody questions them. Coaches do not even have to get their juniors through any playing exams. It is all too easy. When the juniors, or adults, fail, they put it down to their own inability, not the ineffective coaching lessons. To be fair to the coaches, they do not have anything with which to compare their training. I was fortunate to have table tennis, in which I was trained by a brilliant tutor called Keith Summerfield.

It is sad, though, that most coaches do not examine the relevance or effectiveness of their own teaching methods, but then nobody ever asks them to. I am afraid that, in too many cases, coaches do not stand back and assess what they are doing in their lessons, either because they are not professional enough to care, or because they do not know how to.

However, it has to be recognised that some do care, and try to do something about it, and, I am quite sure, find a way of teaching successfully in a few cases, so I congratulate such coaches in the UK – their customers are very lucky to have found them. The truth is, though, it should not be like this – just left to chance as to whether the coaching is good, bad or indifferent.

After over twenty-five years' experience as a full-time coach, I have to say quite honestly, as shocking as it may seem, that someone wishing to learn to play tennis properly from scratch only has about a five to ten percent chance of finding a coach who can achieve this for them. It is interesting that most coaches will tell you they are not impressed with many of the LTA training courses – qualification or otherwise – but they suffer in silence because, unlike me, they want to keep their noses clean and prefer not to rock the boat.

One highly regarded and hard-working coach confided to my co-author that the LTA will not 'nail their colours to the mast' when asked about how to go about teaching a certain aspect of tennis: their stance will usually be one of 'You can do it like this, or you can do it like that', or you can even work it out for yourself. This was in complete contrast to the very precise responses the coach had got during a course he had attended in Spain: 'This is how we do it because we know it works'.

And how many times, when I ask a coach how he would start teaching a ten year-old complete beginner, do I hear: 'Well, it depends'? What they should be able to do is reel off a series of steps they would follow to teach the ten year-old to serve and rally properly on both his forehand and backhand sides, but they never can. I have reached the conclusion, perhaps inevitably, that 'it depends' relates more to how the coach feels on the day rather than what the particular ten year-old actually needs.

The message that I want to convey, therefore, as clearly as I possibly can, is: enough is enough! The LTA coaching system is just not fit for purpose. I can assure you that I have not come up with this conclusion in a matter of weeks or even months – it is, rather, the result of observing from my lowly vantage point what has been going on for many, many years. British tennis will not improve until someone with real knowledge has the courage to take some action.

I have just used the expression 'coaching system', but, perhaps, I should be more precise: the LTA do not have a coaching system. How can this not be the case, when I attended my first thirty six-hour LTA qualification course in 1985 and learnt nothing about how to teach someone to play, and in the last few years qualified coaches have approached me to ask: 'What is the service grip again?'; 'How do you notice when someone's grip has slipped?'; 'What is the split step?'; 'Exactly where should you stand when rallying?'; 'How do you teach the half-volley?'; 'In what order should I coach the strokes and tactics...?'

'Count the balls out, count the balls in' was the only useful piece of advice that a fellow coach could remember when we both reminisced about the above revamped, updated and supposedly much improved Elementary course we had been on together. We laughed at the fact that neither of us could recall any useful coaching tips at all which would benefit anyone we might teach who wished to improve at tennis.

I could go on and on with many more examples of really basic questions from so-called experienced coaches, many of whom had been coaching longer than I had when they sought my help, but my co-author is about to berate me.

In order to convince you that the LTA do not have a system, I can tell you that when such coaches have requested help, I have asked many about how they start coaching a beginner: what they teach first, second, and third, etc. And they all guess at answers, with a few stating: 'It depends'. I have heard this so, so many times. But, when I suggest it is an eight-year old, or an adult, they still do not have an answer.

For a beginner, any beginner, of whatever age, it simply does not depend, and every coach should have a system he can follow to teach his pupil to play. And the reason coaches do not have a system is because they were never given one by the LTA Coaching Department on their courses. I was never given one, either – I had to work it out for myself over a period of time. When I say 'system', I mean a logical order in which to teach the different aspects of tennis so that the pupil will learn to play properly, and, if they have the talent and put the time in, they will have the possibility of developing to a very high level, even a world-class level in some cases. And the logical order I have and use is the system that I have devised myself.

However, I have to emphasise that my system is not the only system – there are many, but a coach, if he is to be successful, simply has to have one. Then, he needs a method by which to teach the various strokes and tactics. None of the coaches who have approached me for some extra training have ever had a system or a method, and have probably never considered devising one. They just coach the player in front of them according to how they feel at the time. And these are the coaches who do care because they have asked me to help them in an effort to improve their knowledge and teaching ability.

Later in this chapter you will read about a coach from the Czech Republic I interviewed, who had both a method and system – quite different to mine – but they were eminently effective at teaching sound basics to the beginners and improvers taking part in the session. No wonder Ivan Lendl and Martina Navratilova became world-class.

At a tennis conference, where I addressed about fifty coaches in my capacity as a Regional Director of the PTR coaching organisation (Professional Tennis Registry), I could not believe that I was the only one who made notes after every lesson. I could not understand how a coach could start lesson five, for example, without referring to what had already been taught in the previous four. I always check my notes for any difficulties encountered, and any other comments I may have made, which are liable to have a significant effect on my approach to lesson five. If you are going to give a pupil the best possible lesson, you simply have to know what has gone before.

Some players, of course, progress more quickly than others, so lesson five for a talented player will be completely different from the one given to a pupil who learns more slowly. The only way I will know which stage each pupil has reached is by referring to the notes I have made about him.

To my mind, this is what a professional coach should do every time. And it is just the same if you are teaching a group. I also often note the method by which a pupil appears to learn the quickest, so that I remember to approach the next lesson in the most effective way possible for that particular pupil. I should point out here that I am not trying to show you how wonderful I am because I always keep notes about those I teach – it just seems normal to me.

The aim of this book is to get us out of the mess we are in, and therefore improve the state of British tennis: if fully-qualified coaches in the UK do not see the need to keep notes, then this is yet another indication of how amateur we are. How can a junior, or adult beginner, make progress if there is no careful monitoring of that progress by the coach. It is like teaching and learning in a vacuum. An Ofsted inspector would have a fit if the teachers in a particular school just taught according to their whims, with no regard for the syllabus or specifications. Of course, in British tennis, there is no syllabus, or anything remotely like it.

Coming back to me, and I am not showing off, I have kept notes from day one as a coach because I considered it impossible to teach without them. Despite my attending countless training courses, nobody ever suggested I should keep notes. That is the shocking truth of the matter, and is another example of the poor training given to prospective coaches. Perhaps I should not be surprised, therefore, that other coaches have never considered keeping notes. Maybe it is easy for me because I have a coaching method, system, and structure which are all explained to those I teach in my literature. Perhaps my more professional training as a table tennis coach has something to do with it. It is worth repeating because it is so important: the LTA do not have a method, syllabus, or system – it is therefore hardly surprising that such things are not uppermost in the minds of coaches when they qualify.

In truth, it is not the coaches I blame for giving lessons that leave so much to be desired, but those who trained them, or, to be more precise, those who passed them, handing them certificates that said they were fully-qualified to teach tennis. Without being patronising but just honest, when it comes to making notes, many coaches probably do not understand what they should be writing anyway. Some coaches tell me that they do not see any need to keep notes, and others say that they can remember everything from previous lessons.

My USPTR tutor, Piers Bastard, used to refer to tennis lessons as 'tennis clinics' because, just as doctors cure medical ailments, so coaches should cure tennis ones. Now, doctors would not dream of not keeping notes, so why should coaches be any different? Schoolteachers also keep notes, often copious, about their pupils – they could not teach properly without them. My co-author, who is a retired schoolteacher, assures me that this is so throughout the profession. What I do, therefore, is standard, or, at least, should be standard – it is nothing special. Otherwise, we had better consider every doctor and teacher as special, rather than just doing their jobs properly.

In order to illustrate how important it is for a tennis coach to make notes, I can relate the following, but looking back, I do have to smile at myself for feeling so guilty about an evening's coaching I had to do. The problem with me is, I am just too serious – I could even pass for a German.

I was travelling to coach at a school once, and suddenly came over hot and cold just before arriving. I got myself into quite a state, which is why I remember it so well, and also for the guilt I felt that day while coaching. The reason for my anxiety was that I realised I had forgotten to take my school coaching manual containing the students' notes. Not having my timetable either did not matter, as there was one on the school notice board I could refer to, and, in any case, I knew all the girls would know to turn up for their lessons as normal. But their coaching notes. I spent five minutes waiting for the first girl – Rebecca – to arrive, thinking about what exactly I should teach her.

I knew Rebecca had attended about four lessons, but had I combined her forehand and backhand drives yet? Had I started rallying with her? And was this from the service line or the baseline? Perhaps I had not completed the technique for her backhand drive yet? Was this the girl I discussed possibly trying single-handed rather than double-handed in future? Was it Rebecca who specifically asked me last time to help her a little more with one of her strokes before moving on? I was stuck, with every reason to panic. There was only one course of action, I decided: first, I would ask her if she had any requests or preferences, and, if she did not, then I would start teaching her to serve, since I knew she had never done this. I made notes on a spare sheet of paper for all my lessons that day, and then wrote them up in my manual when I got home. I was disappointed, though not surprised, to discover that I had slightly messed up the progress of a couple of the girls.

I hope that this gives you an idea of why coaching notes are invaluable. Why not ask any coaches you know if they make notes after every lesson they give? Or, if you are attending coaching yourself, or your offspring is, ask to see the notes on the lessons the coach has given. I will be very surprised if the coach can show you anything like a complete set of notes if, that is, he can show you any notes at all.

One tennis-playing father of a youngster I had coached for a year asked me what his daughter had learnt so far. I was able to go through the list and order of everything I had covered from my notes, and he left very happy. I am sure, though, that this was nothing more than he expected from me. And why not? I was her coach, and it was only right that I had a record of the stage she had reached with her tennis. I had not done anything special – I just carried out my coaching to the best of my ability.

It has to be said that, sadly, in the make-it-fun approach of LTA tennis coaching, the above angst on my part at forgetting my students' notes would not register at all – it would, in fact, be supremely irrelevant. 'Just get the pupils running round and doing some agility exercises; play some fun games...' I can hear the tutor saying.

This brings me back to the American tennis article I referred to in Chapter 4, in which the journalist could not fathom out what was wrong with British tennis, having analysed it from all angles – culture, climate, population, funding, etc. If you remember, it was an exhaustive study of the situation in the UK, comparing it to that in other countries, and the conclusion was that the UK had more than enough in its favour to produce many more top players. The writer simply could not understand why Britain failed so miserably. At least he recognised that Britain certainly had a problem.

However, while the analysis was certainly very thorough, there was one crucial aspect that was missed when the LTA Coaching Department was examined. The writer only looked at the surface, making reference to the wonderful coaching qualification structure that existed, and the many extra training courses on offer to coaches. He even mentioned the marvellous glossy brochures advertising the courses. I could clearly see how he had got it wrong: he had obviously not experienced these marvellous courses in the way a coach would, religiously attending every session. While the glossy brochures, the refreshments, and the welcome at training courses made everything seem very professional and impressive to the American journalist,

I can assure you – and him – that the actual content of the courses nearly always falls woefully short of such promising beginnings and appearances.

How many examples of bad training do you want me to give? Of course, if I am right about this, then you may well ask why many other coaches seem to accept these LTA courses without demur. I certainly do not, because I do not enjoy wasting my valuable time, as well as knowing it is costing me money to hear so many irrelevant, misleading, or inaccurate comments. Quite often the tutors look to those attending for ideas on how they currently coach, advertise, or whatever, so we end up hearing what we collectively know already, which is not inspiring in the least.

One prominent tennis club member I was sitting next to at a seminar offered a seemingly clever way to welcome new members to a club with a view to retaining them in the long term. 'I like that solution,' said the tutor with a smile. 'Put that one at the top of your list, everyone, that's a good idea.' I was less sure of how successful my neighbour's suggestion would turn out to be, so I quietly questioned him about it afterwards. 'Oh no,' he responded, 'we tried it at our club once and it was a real flop, but I thought I'd mention the idea since they wanted some suggestions.'

So all those on the training course left that day convinced that his suggestion for attracting players to join a club long term was very good. Why did the tutor not immediately know that the suggestion was flawed, or, at the very least, question the soundness of the idea? The tutor obviously did not know his subject. And, considering that virtually all the ideas the tutor wrote up on his board came from the coaches, it was those attending who taught those attending in that particular lecture – the tutor contributed next to nothing.

As an on-court coaching example at another seminar I attended, a cross-court baseline drill was set up of forehand to forehand for top-class juniors. Two ex-professional players from our group offered to follow the tutor's instructions and do the forehand drill demonstration. They were brilliant players, and I waited to see what advice we, the coaches, would be given as to how to develop them further, especially since they already had a high playing standard. I waited for such suggestions as 'Make sure the players are recovering back into position properly', or 'Check to see if your opponent has failed to recover his position and, if so, go down the line', or 'Look for the short ball and then hit harder and flatter into the gap for a possible winner', or 'When and how to hit behind your opponent', or 'When to take the ball early and on the rise', and many other ideas I had in mind.

But what was the advice given by our former Davis Cup player presenting this drill? 'Now come on, put some oomph into it, both of you,' and 'Let's see the topspin.' I can, though, assure you that the former professional players demonstrating the drill were top-spinning more than adequately.

I felt very depressed at the irrelevance of the advice from the tutor, and equally depressed that the coaches around me were actually writing 'Put some oomph into it' on their notepads. How ironic: coaches take notes when they would do better not to, and do not take notes when there is a real need. Not one coaching tip was given, except when someone asked what you should do if your juniors cannot control the ball as well as the demonstrators. And the advice given was to get them to rally from the service line only, until they gained better control before returning to the desired baseline rally again.

However, any properly trained coach will tell you

that anyone who cannot control the ball that well from the baseline will almost certainly have a flaw in their technique. A player with poor technique will not correct it by just playing on a smaller court, but will just reinforce the fault. In fact, rallying from the service line will hide the technical flaw to an extent, thus making it more difficult to detect and put right.

This is what I mean by incorrect advice, and yet this time it was coming from a so-called top tutor in our sport. The problem is that he was an ex-Davis Cup player, and not a coach or tutor. As has been pointed out before, coaching is one thing, playing professionally is another. In a fierce cross-court rally in a match, our ex-Davis Cup man would have done the right things to try and gain the upper hand in the point, but he would have done it all by instinct, and instinct is not sufficient to make you a competent coach.

I could give you many more examples, but I can only think that coaches are taken in by these training ideas, because, as I have already explained, they have become conditioned to this unproductive type of tuition from when they were coached as juniors, and then from attending their own qualification courses; in any case, they do not dare to question the distinguished tutors who give the advice. And, above all, having received such inept training, they are desperate for something else to say in their lessons. So, if a former top British player says 'put some oomph into it', then it must be worth using and will add variety to their next lesson.

While I have attended some excellent lectures over the years, as well as my seventeen-day qualification course delivered by the outstanding Kenyan, Piers Bastard, I have to say that, when it comes to extra training as described above with the forehand to forehand cross-court rally, I find too often that the advice given is either irrelevant, or misleading, or just plain mediocre.

Before the LTA licence became of paramount importance, I was allowed to be a tutor for Kent and ran a half-day training course for coaches. I was given the freedom to cover any aspect of tennis I chose, and, on one occasion, while contemplating what I would talk about, I received a telephone call from one of the attendees asking me if I could cover the right order a coach should teach the various strokes and tactics of the game. In my own teaching of tennis I call this 'The Coaching System', and I decided to make it the subject of my lecture.

About six coaches attended, and I started going through a logical and effective order that I generally follow when coaching, although, it has to be said, there is not just one order. However, early on in the lecture, when explaining about the fundamentals of the forehand drive before ensuring that topspin can be imparted, I saw the totally mystified look on the experienced coaches' faces in front of me.

'The left hand does what?' and 'What did you mean about the angle of the racquet?' were just two of the questions now being asked, and it quickly became evident that none of them knew the fundamentals for teaching one of the basic strokes in tennis. Their knowledge of this stroke was limited to 'low to high' and 'contact in front', and I found myself having to explain absolute basics to them all – it was as if they were attending my adult beginners' class. But then I should not have been surprised because, from all the LTA courses I have attended teaching me anything about technique, it has always been limited to: grip the racquet like so, and it is a throwing action for the serve; swing from low to high, contact in front, for the groundstrokes; and punch for the volley. But you have to ask: if this is all there is to it, who needs a coach to learn how to play tennis?

Out on the court most of them had very good-looking strokes, but they had no idea of what they did or how they did it, let alone how to teach it to a beginner. At the end of the lecture I was asked: 'Where did you learn all this?' and the following comment was made as well: 'I've never learnt so much in just three hours'. It is nice to be complimented, but the obvious question to be asked now is: why did the coaches know so little? You probably know the answer already.

I once came across an LTA coach who had the highest qualifications possible and a very good playing standard. The problem was that he never said anything at all to his juniors when coaching them. His pupils told me he would rally with them individually, which they enjoyed, but the only sound that ever came from his lips was either a polite chuckle, or a little song. Quite surprised at this, I asked: 'What did he sing?' 'Oh, it was always the same thing,' replied one of the older teenagers, whose name was Annabel. 'Whenever I missed the ball, he'd sing: "There's a hole in your racquet, dear Annabel, dear Annabel, there's a hole in your racquet, dear Annabel, a hole".' I am sure you know the catchy tune that goes with, 'There's a hole in your bucket'.

At the time, there was only one other coach in the whole county who could match this man's qualifications, and yet, Annabel still played like a beginner with not a hope of completing a six-stroke rally after three years of individual coaching with him. She had no technique, had never made a grip change, and had honestly not learnt a thing. At least, this top coach introduced a bit of fun and made her laugh when she missed the ball.

I ask the following question: does this level of teaching exist in any other form of education in this country? And, what would the Germans make of it all? Or anybody else, for that matter? Of course, as already stated, I obtained my LTA qualification back in 1985, so you might expect the British approach to coaching to have improved since then, especially since the LTA have updated, changed and added to their courses with great frequency over the last thirty years or so. I am sorry to report, though, that there has been no such improvement. I have attended many other training courses much more recently, and, from time to time, I also sit down, out of interest, with newly-qualified coaches to talk to them about their latest LTA training.

'A waste of time' or 'not very good' are the two most common descriptions I hear, and I have started to work out why so many coaches describe their courses, especially the accreditation ones, in this way. I believe it is because, without any actual system or method to use for the teaching of tennis, they cannot see where any extra training they receive fits in – it just leads to confusion.

One coach I had trained with my system and method for teaching tennis described one of his 'Accreditation' training days or 'Continuous Professional Development' (CPD) as 'not very good', but explained to me that he was not worried because he felt confident about how he coached anyway, and could ignore all the irrelevant and misleading information being taught that day, which he said was at least 90% of the course. He added that there were a couple of bits worth listening to, and he did enjoy the day, but then so he should, since he was only twenty-one at the time – at that age, meeting new people and having new experiences are per se exciting – just wait till he gets to my age.

While you may think that the comments I constantly make, both here and elsewhere, are rather harsh, all I am doing is reporting on what other coaches have told me, and on what I have experienced myself.

The simple fact of the matter is: there is a lot to teaching tennis and much to learn, but, from the very many training (CPD) and qualification courses that are, and have been, in existence, I find it remarkable, to say the least, that so little content is geared to what a customer really needs. For example: how do I hit with topspin like the pros?; how do I get the ball over the net time and time again?; how do I get those fast balls back?; and many other considerations, all requiring very precise teaching.

To give yet another example of how unsatisfactory it all is, not long ago, a young coach was talking to me about the recent LTA qualification course he had just passed, and I was interested in how he had been taught to coach the serve. There ensued a long pause while he thought about my question. I told him that he was probably going to be coaching the serve on a beginners' course that he was about to give at the local club. There was yet more hesitation and frowning from him, before he murmured at last: 'Well, they didn't really explain anything to me about the serve. Perhaps they ignored me as I have a very good serve, and some of the other coaches on my course didn't.'

Quite possibly, I thought, as he was certainly right about the fact that he himself had a great serve. But how well one coach can serve compared to another is not the issue here: it is, rather, how a coach teaches his pupils to serve properly that matters. So I asked him again how he would be teaching the serve when he took his imminent junior beginners' course, especially as I now knew that he had not been taught how to do it – would he be capable of coming up with something? He finally replied: 'I don't really know – I suppose I'll think of something when the time comes'.

How can we go on subjecting juniors and adult beginners to such treatment? It is just too unprofessional for words. No wonder the LTA are so keen on Cardio tennis – at least, then, you do not have to worry about teaching technique – just let them give the low-compression ball 'a whack' (R. Draper, Radio 5 Live, 2013) and it miraculously stays in the court. And everybody has FUN and cannot wait for the next session.

But what about the serious junior beginner who really wants to learn and goes along to his local club for lessons? He may well have the potential to take tennis to the very highest level, but, with things as they are at present, his chances of doing so are nil – he might as well not bother, and would do far better to go and try out a sport that has proper coaching and guidance.

Of course, I fully recognise that there will be a few coaches who have worked out a successful way to teach tennis, but you will have to be very lucky to have found such a coach: whatever happens, do not give up on such a precious commodity and look elsewhere because you will be doomed to mediocrity again, if not worse.

Then we come to how much time a coach has to spend getting his qualifications. If we accept that teachers, doctors, dentists, etc. have to spend years learning their skills before they can practise, then why should the profession of tennis coach be thought of so differently? In the not too distant past, it was virtually a question of hours, let alone weeks or months or even, perish the thought, years.

Learning to coach on an LTA course could take no more than a few days, and certainly not much more than a week of actual training. But, worse than the LTA, were the two other recognised coaching organisations in this country, through which, for over twenty years, you could gain a qualification in just four days, with the exam on the fifth day.

To be fair, the content of the four-day qualification course was very good, but, unfortunately, it was far too short for anyone to have a chance of coming away with sufficient knowledge and confidence to coach properly.

The situation now, as long as the system has not changed yet again, is that the LTA have in the last few years lengthened the time it takes to become qualified. It all takes longer because the courses are fitted in over a period of six months, a year, or even two years. However, it is still unsatisfactory for a so-called profession – the reality is that the actual training boils down to just a matter of weeks, let alone months or years. From the way the LTA website reads it is all very impressive, but when one delves below the surface, a different story emerges.

The other two organisations have complicated their qualification processes, not for the better, in my opinion, realising that they need to conform with certain LTA requirements in order to continue attracting candidates to their own courses in the UK.

What the LTA have done is introduce an extra dimension by requiring candidates to spend some time, during the six-month, one-year, or two-year period, gaining practical experience on court with highly-qualified coaches who probably trained under the old, shorter regimes.

It all looks good, or, at least, it looks better than before, but, since the content generally of the courses has left so much to be desired over the years, and still leaves so much to be desired, even though the courses are longer now, one has to question whether the training that goes on really prepares a coach to teach anyone to play tennis properly.

And as regards the extra dimension of on-court experience with a highly-qualified coach, I have the following to recount.

An ex-pupil of mine, of a very good playing standard, had the opportunity to earn some money as a coach at a commercial centre, even though he had never qualified as a coach, or even tried to. (Please see 'The Solution' for more comment on the employment of unqualified coaches.) He therefore came to me for some help and advice which I gave him over a period of a few months. After management changes at the centre which did not suit him, he decided to attend an LTA qualification course in order to be able to get a job elsewhere. For his on-court practical experience, he would have liked to continue with me, but he had to go to an LTA coach who held qualifications that I did not possess.

The problem was that his mentor was unprofessional in the extreme, and my ex-pupil simply could not believe his eyes: he turned up late, literally every time, for his first adult individual lesson of the day; used a mixture of ball types; had no notes to refer to for his customers – not surprising; and only made vague coaching comments which had no effect at all on the strokes of his pupils. After training from me, my former pupil realised fully just how utterly useless his LTA coach and mentor was.

I hope that, by now, you are beginning to realise that there are very good reasons why our juniors find it extremely difficult, or even impossible, to become world-class. The simple reality is that the coaching system is a mess because any previous good techniques and teaching points that might have existed have got lost in a morass of other things: in short, confusion, rather than clarity, has become the order of the day. Our coaches do not stand a chance, therefore, which, in turn, means that our juniors do not stand a chance. I cannot put it more plainly than that.

I found it interesting that, in designing a manual on the procedure for a coach to follow when taking groups, I broke it down into nine stages. And when I checked it through, the most critical considerations for eight of the nine stages had never been taught to me on any of the many courses I have attended. This example in itself is a clear indication of how the relevant and important points that should be taught to coaches, and very much used every time when delivering lessons, are missed.

A number of coaches do incorporate some of these key considerations because they have obviously worked them out for themselves, as I had to, but it should not be left to chance like this – it should all be made clear in their training. What is the point of skilled people attending so-called professional training when they find themselves having to devise different methods to those taught on their courses in order to do their jobs properly?

Also of relevance to this gravest of problems is the fact that, quite often, newly-qualified coaches, and some quite experienced ones too, having heard good reports about me, travel from their workplaces to meet me for training purposes on a particular aspect of coaching. Sadly, they are all so lacking in some of the basics of teaching tennis, that not only would I not allow my son or daughter ever to have a lesson with many of them, but I would actually invite these coaches to take up a place on my adults' beginners course. Fully-qualified coaches, with years of experience, who have assisted me on my six-hour beginners' course, have all been shocked at how much they have learnt, and how much they did not know that really matters.

This is what I mean by coaches constantly receiving training on peripheral aspects, but not being taught what is essential for everyday, basic coaching. Once again, it is a reality issue. The simple truth is: you cannot blame the coaches for the way they teach – you can only blame the tutors on their training courses. My co-author informs me that I have mentioned this many times before, but, then, I am not perfect like what he is.

But let me assure you once again that I have only seen through it all because of my particularly analytical and logical approach to coaching tennis; the fact that I had never had a tennis lesson myself; and also the fact that I had received training from a table tennis coach which was much more methodical and precise, as it also was on my first non-LTA course from Piers Bastard.

I would never have been able to sort out a reasonable tennis coaching method and system for myself without this background, and I would still be guessing and endlessly searching for answers, just like many British coaches are doing, and have been doing for years, up and down the country. In truth, I am sure that being in such an unenviable position would have made me give up within five years, and I would have returned to my boring job at the Ministry of Defence and the wonders of the IT world.

It is also important to point out that poor coaching seems to be endemic in the UK, and can be found in all parts of the coaching spectrum. I can refer to the numerous coaching sections over the years in tennis magazines to highlight many more examples of irrelevant or inaccurate coaching tips.

On the couple of occasions that I saw fit to complain to the LTA about misleading tips in the British tennis magazine called *Ace*, I was brushed aside by the Coaching Department because, according to them, they had nothing to do with the contents of the magazine in question. Initially, I thought that this was a fair enough response, if it were indeed the case, but, upon reflection, I would question why they did not seem concerned on hearing that inaccurate coaching tips were being given to many British tennis enthusiasts through the number one monthly tennis publication in the UK at the time.

However, despite the LTA's stance with regard to the magazine, one such tip in *Ace* from several years ago is worth recalling, since, on this occasion, it was given by staff from the LTA Coaching Department.

The tip was about the double-handed backhand drive. Amanda Coetzer, a regular top 10 player for many years, was used to illustrate the shot. The LTA Coaching Department attempted to show the grip Amanda was using, but placed the demonstrator's hands on the racquet handle differently to the way Amanda had hers. In telephoning the LTA Coaching Department to point this out, the lady I spoke to admitted it was actually her hands being photographed to illustrate the grip. And she was rather intrigued by my call, since she told me she had wondered at the time if the Head Coach had positioned her hands correctly, as she was an LTA-qualified coach herself. We discussed it for several minutes, and the lady came to see clearly how different her grip was from Amanda Coetzer's.

It was, of course, too late for any correction to be made – the damage had already been done, and thousands of juniors were now being persuaded to swing at their backhands like Amanda Coetzer with not a hope of success.

What a sorry state we are in when even the LTA Coaching

Department cannot get things right. Is it any wonder that our coaches do not deliver? In my opinion and, perhaps, in yours as well, such a mistake is absolutely unforgivable. I was grateful at least for the LTA member of staff's honesty and the fact that she thanked me for my call.

As I have made clear before in the book, I only want to help and improve British tennis: if I criticise a lot, it is because there is a lot to criticise. Whether I am ultimately thanked for my efforts does not really matter – all I want is for changes to be made for the better.

Apart from magazines, thoroughly misleading tips can also be seen on coaching videos. One such example is worthy of reporting, since it was presented by the Head of the LTA Coaching Department himself. He attempted to give the viewer some useful advice on 'the forehand' – he should have said 'the forehand drive', of course – after having a professional player demonstrate the shot perfectly. He then explained what he thought were the two most common faults for this stroke for the average recreational player. Standing on the court in place of the professional, the Head of the Coaching Department allowed the ball approaching him literally to hit his leg, and announced that many players let the ball get too close to their body. The next ball he then allowed to pass him, out of the reach of his racquet, exclaiming: 'Or they swing at the ball with it too far away from them'.

As a coach with more than twenty-five years' experience, I can assure you that neither of these faults is at all common. In fact, it is a rarity for either to occur. I could name six far more common problems with the forehand drive, which I see many times every week, but the coach on the video – the LTA Head of Coaching, no less – had actually come out with a thoroughly irrelevant piece of advice which was not going to help anyone, all very similar to the current CPD Accreditation Courses.

I do, however, recognise that it is just about possible for these two problems to occur, but the two faults he highlighted are both judgement problems, which cannot be coached, rather than technical ones, which can be.

This is, in fact, a very good example of the LTA being completely out of touch with reality at grass-roots level, which is where the average recreational player, the target of the LTA video, would be playing, and perhaps desperately trying to improve.

Moreover, I would suggest that his sole reason for giving such an irrelevant tip was that he could not honestly think of anything else to say – he just literally dreamt something up which he thought sounded reasonable. I can be fairly certain that he did not really know the technical elements required to play the forehand drive, otherwise he would have very usefully referred to some of them.

And the trouble is, anyone trying to learn from this video would then get rather too concerned with the distance they stand from the ball, and this would start to inhibit their judgement and movement, when previously they had always got into the right position. So the chances are, this tip would make a player worse! And that is LTA coaching for you from the very top in a nutshell, and in a video.

My co-author tells me that I could rest my case here, but, on this occasion, I am ignoring him. I have put up with all this for too many years to let it go now, and, anyway, I have some very good examples coming up of what is fundamentally wrong with British tennis.

So here we go again.

In an article in a British tennis magazine, the writer asked twenty top coaches from around the country what they considered to be the most common fault with the average club or recreational player. In my opinion, all twenty coaches, or nearly all, should have been in agreement, but they were not. There were a few replies that agreed on the same fault, which was the quite common one of standing in the wrong place on a tennis court, but only one coach actually came up with the correct answer.

The fault in question is, from the technical point of view, the one that, above all others, halts a player's progress the most. I mention it several times every day when coaching beginners or recreational players, and, if you visit a mix-in at a tennis club, you will notice that this is the most common and serious fault of all. The only person who came up with the answer was Paul Davey, someone I happen to know well and admire as a very good coach.

It is particularly significant, for the purposes of this book, that out of twenty top coaches, nineteen were unaware of this major problem for grass-roots players, and, believe me, from where I come from, it IS the overwhelmingly right answer to the question. For your edification, and I am taking the liberty here of assuming that you do not know, the most common fault at this level of tennis is holding the racquet with the wrong grip. Interestingly, according to a top coaching magazine, published a few years ago in the USA, over 80% of recreational players serve with the wrong grip.

This one example illustrates perfectly why I attribute the mess we are in to what is happening at grass-roots level: it goes without saying that many youngsters start playing in such circumstances – i.e. in sessions with players holding the racquet wrongly and, more important, with coaches seemingly unaware of how to recognise that the grip has not changed or slipped. Quite simply, it is all down to very poor training, resulting in an alarming ignorance of the mechanics of tennis and a complete lack of professionalism.

To illustrate further – my co-author comments that I do love doing this, and I reply that it does have a purpose – I relate the following:

While waiting for a friend to finish an individual lesson, I observed how he recognised that his twelve year-old pupil was trying to play backhand volleys with the wrong grip, and corrected him, before moving to the baseline to feed him balls so that he could practise the shot. But, by the time my friend had fed the first ball, the lad had changed his grip back to a most inappropriate one, quite unintentionally, I am sure – probably because the correct grip given to him did not feel very comfortable.

Ten minutes of horrible-looking backhand volleys ensued, with the coach shouting encouragement and corrections which could not help in any way until the boy adopted the right grip.

Afterwards, I told my friend what had happened. 'Really?' he exclaimed, 'the little blighter, I'll look out for that next time. Thank you.'

But did the pupil receive a refund for my friend's incompetence, and why should this coach notice the next time, if he did not spot the problem the first time? And has this twelve year-old, by practising with the wrong grip, now got into an irretrievably bad volleying habit?

This is just one example of unacceptable practice: ironically, the coach did at least spot the main problem at the very start, but he did not have the ability to see that it was still happening. The question has to be asked: is there no proper testing of how to coach the volley on qualification courses?

On my way to the Eastbourne championships one year, the fellow coach I was with wanted to look in at a nearby club. A lesson was just starting and the Head Professional was saying to a group of ladies: 'To serve properly, you must use the chopper grip and then it is nice and easy'. He then proceeded to demonstrate the shot by hitting effortless, 'nice and easy' serves down the court. But, although he showed his group of ladies the chopper grip, by the time they were serving, six out of eight of them had lost it, and serving was anything but 'nice and easy'.

Three messages I am trying to get across in writing this chapter can be seen in this one simple example of substandard coaching:

1. The coach was right to point out the grip to use, but did not notice that 75% of his group did not retain it;
2. The comment of 'nice and easy' does not teach anything to beginners;
3. In the strict professional sense, coaching notes should be made, but what notes can you make from such an uninformative and bland lesson?

There is one last, additional comment I would like to make about the above : 'nice and easy' as an instruction is quite inappropriate, since it implies one should be relaxed, and the more relaxed the ladies became, the more out of control they were with their serves. There are so many other useful tips the coach could have given, but was he simply unaware of the techniques for serving, or was he not in the mood to put in the hard work that day?

Moreover, serving with the wrong grip can lead to the dreaded injury known as 'tennis elbow', which all coaches should be very mindful of.

Unfortunately, there is an extra dimension to the problem we have in Great Britain with coaches who do not know their trade: bad coaching is far worse than no coaching at all. So many, by making faulty diagnoses, are actually making our juniors play worse than they would do if they had been left to their own devices. This is because, when a player steps on to the court for the first time and has a go, he is highly unlikely to hit technically perfect serves, drives and volleys. But, what he does do, is swing in a way that feels natural to him. That is to say, he will swing the way his body wants to swing, whether this is technically right or wrong, and it will probably be based upon mental pictures he has formed from watching Wimbledon.

The result may be poor in the strict technical sense, and is also likely to be poor in terms of controlling the ball, but the swing will feel relatively easy, flowing and comfortable, even if not that effective. Now, the correct technique is also natural for the body to execute, and will feel easy and comfortable once you have practised it for a short time, even if it does not feel comfortable straightaway.

Just ask any high-standard tennis player if they feel comfortable with their strokes, and they will invariably tell you that they do. So there are two wonderfully smooth and natural techniques for our body to use: first, the way your body wants to swing naturally before any interference, and, secondly, the correct technique after good coaching, even though it may take time to feel natural, since your body initially fights the new swing paths which seem to go against your body's natural instincts.

The reason for changing to the correct technique, incidentally, is because, with few exceptions, it is the only way to be very effective in terms of consistency, accuracy, power and spin. The correct technique also has the added bonus of not causing an injury. But what happens if your natural technique is replaced with an unnatural one, but which is also not the correct technique? You will now be forcing your body to swing in neither its natural way, nor in the most effective way.

This unnatural and incorrect technique is more likely to make you prone to injury, and you will also be building incorrect muscle memory which will just become more and more ingrained, and more difficult to change should you ever be later taught correctly.

We are getting into seriously dangerous territory here, from which it can become impossible to recover. But this is sadly what is happening much of the time on the coaching front. This one observation on its own about playing tennis is enough to make you appreciate the incredible importance of quality coaching from day one.

If you are unlucky enough to be born in the UK, you have probably realised by now that it is easy to acquire bad technical habits, but, curiously, a four-day junior coaching course I once happened to come across at a local club certainly ensured that no one was going to suffer in this way.

I turned up on the third day and observed forty children in four groups of ten playing team games. On one court the team were throwing tennis balls at chairs placed near the net; another court had them playing hockey using their tennis racquets; on a third court the children had to dodge tennis balls being hit at them by the coaches; and on the fourth court another general PE-type game was in progress, but, just like the others, had no relation to learning how to play tennis. After twenty minutes a whistle was blown and the four teams rotated round.

Now, is it just me, or would you not also expect these children to be learning a tennis stroke, or how to rally by the third day? Certainly, a friend of mine, who I noticed was assisting on the course, revealed later to me that he was astounded no actual tuition was given as to how to play tennis throughout the four days. The four team games, all of which the children seemed to be enjoying – undoubtedly it was FUN – are games I have also used on my beginners' courses, but I use just one of them for the first five to ten minutes of a session. The rest of the time I teach beginners how to play the forehand and backhand drives, how to serve, and how to move and rally properly. Is this not what my customers would expect and want?

And it was not just from this course that I heard disgruntled parents saying that they did not feel their children had learnt very much – I was always being told that they learnt so much more, and made far better progress, when attending my courses. I suppose it is hardly surprising when one considers that I was the only coach actually teaching them the techniques for the basic strokes in tennis.

I must make it clear that I am not looking for any praise by reporting this fact, but just informing you that I simply got on with teaching tennis from day one, which, after all, was what I was being paid to do, while most other coaches concentrated, and still concentrate now, on fun racquet-and-ball games a huge percentage of the time, and, furthermore, they think that this is correct, and that it is what the children want. What I do though, is simple, and could so easily be taught to all coaches.

There is, however, another reason for coaches working in this way: they do not have a system or method for teaching someone to play from scratch, and they do not have sufficient knowledge either to develop them further so that they can learn to play to a higher standard. They therefore just ensure that the children have fun, using the many games and drills they have learnt on their training courses. The mind boggles at what they move these children on to after completing their six-hour beginners' courses, or, in some cases, even ten-hour courses.

Now, you may well protest vigorously at what I am saying, telling me that you are having coaching and are definitely improving. In answer to this, I first have to say there is a 5-10% chance that you are one of the lucky ones who actually has a good coach. But, for all the others, I ask the following: is it that you rally better because of the confidence-boosting comments your coach shouts down the court, and the fact that he sends you a perfect ball to hit each time?

Then there is the fact that there is less pressure on you continually to hit the ball in than when you hit to a practice partner. And how do you fare in matches? Just by playing over many years, you will be improving. But improving what? You are really just learning how to cope better with the unorthodox strokes you have developed, which limit what you can do, compared to someone with correct technique.

So, your improvement is not necessarily the result of good coaching, but, rather, the result of much practice, and adapting the strokes a little in your own natural way, in order to gain some consistency. And the credit, unbelievably, goes to the coach.

To explain what I mean more clearly, I ask the following question: how many golfers ever complete their very first round in under 100 strokes? Not many, but, without coaching, it is still easy to improve by several shots after just a few rounds, because you are learning how to improve your own way of swinging the club through trial and error, and are becoming more and more familiar with your own golf swing.

But, like tennis, if you are serious about your sport and have ambitions of turning professional and possibly reaching the top, or just trying to be the very best that you are capable of, you cannot compromise on technique – you simply have to work hard on perfecting it very early on.

Why get into bad habits first, which you will only have to undo at a later date? It makes eminent sense to get off to the right start, and this is exactly what our young British tennis players do not get the chance to do. The stark reality is that their technique remains faulty from day one because they are not taught properly.

When coaches have come to me for some training, I often ask them to demonstrate how they would coach one of my customers. They usually conduct a most harmonious lesson, with the customer quite happy with what has taken place. But they never argue with me when, afterwards, I point out to them that they hardly offered a word of advice, technical or otherwise, in half an hour of coaching.

And the coaches accept, once it is explained to them, that they have only been supplying pleasant commentary, with a few jokes and encouraging words thrown in for good measure, and any real coaching advice, if offered at all, has been too vague for anyone to understand or make any difference. In short, the whole session has consisted of nothing more than a load of 'white noise' that served very little purpose.

In tennis, a coach may be able to advise on fitness, tactics or the mental side of the game, but if he cannot coach technically, then he is really not fit to teach tennis, because 80% of coaching is technical until a player actually gets to professional level.

One particular coach I recall, who came to assist me with an adult class, helped by feeding balls alongside me from the net for the customers to practise their groundstrokes. While I gave advice every time that was tailored for each player, so that a technical change was possible for the next attempt at the shot, my new assistant found it impossible to do the same. Despite my instructions to him to give everyone only technical advice, all I heard him saying was: 'Oh, bad luck', 'Oh, try again', 'Just out', 'Oh, nearly', 'Yes, well done' and 'Go on, go on'. This is what I mean by coaches giving 'pleasant commentary' or 'white noise', because it is certainly not coaching, and yet, this is generally, and sadly what all too frequently goes on.

'Yes, well done' may sound appropriate to a casual onlooker, but it is definitely not right – in fact, most of the time it is thoroughly inappropriate, and even inept. 'Well done' what? The ball went in? But the player can see that for himself without the coach telling him. And if the player has played the shot properly, then it makes sense to ensure he knows what it is exactly he has done that has enabled him to be successful on that particular occasion. After all, he wants to be able to repeat it.

During the break between lessons, I pointed out to my assistant the ineffective coaching he was giving, and he was absolutely horrified with himself. It dawned on him for the first time in years of coaching, I might add, that he was not helping anyone at all by teaching in this way. When I asked what he might be looking for in a sound forehand or backhand drive, it further dawned on him that he did not really know. To put it quite simply: if you do not know what constitutes a sound forehand drive, how can you teach it?

Does it surprise you that I exclaim: what a mess we are in.

You might remark, however, that it is better to receive encouraging commentary than incorrect advice, but here is a good example of how safety can be compromised through commentary alone.

On the last two occasions that I have happened to watch coaches teaching the overhead smash, players have fallen over, much to their embarrassment, and have actually apologised for their clumsiness, but, in fact, it was the coaches' fault that they fell over: if they had not been so encouraging, or, even better, had given the correct technical advice, these accidents would have been avoided.

There is, as any competent coach should know, one vital tip to give to ensure that falling over is not a likely outcome when going back for the overhead smash. But the two coaches I was observing made no mention of this, and the encouragement they both gave to their customers to move more quickly in order to get to the ball going over their heads virtually ensured that the mishap would occur.

Why did neither of these qualified coaches emphasise the one vital piece of safety advice for the overhead smash? Had they both forgotten, or was it that they were never taught in the first place when qualifying as coaches? And anyway, were they ever tested on their ability to coach the smash during their training? I can assure you that the answer is almost certainly no.

As I have already stated, qualification courses are not only too short in duration, but are also short on basic, realistic content: there is so much to learn in practical terms, if you want to be a proper, professional tennis coach, that those who put the courses together simply cannot afford to waste time on peripheral and non-essential matters. The syllabus has to be tight and always appropriate for teaching at grass-roots level and above, otherwise those who take lessons miss out, incredibly, in my view, on the very basic things that they need: i.e. learning quickly and efficiently how to get the ball over the net with a technique that is akin to what top players do; in addition, I would imagine, they do not want to be exposed to dangerous situations on the court that could lead to injury – this also is a most basic of requirements.

In case you are wondering what the safety advice should be from a properly trained coach when teaching the smash or, if you are a player, and you want to know how to stop falling over, I give you the following, free of charge: the first move you should make when the lob goes up is to turn sideways; for the right-hander, just pull your right leg, arm and side back – this allows you to move towards the baseline in a sideways-on position, which is the correct position for executing the smash, as well as allowing you to move far more quickly and, most importantly, from a safety point of view, it stops you trying to run and lean backwards, which is always liable to make you lose your balance.

If you can stand it – I know that my co-author most certainly would not be able to, and, remember, taking a regular break from this chapter is definitely advisable – here is yet another example of coaching that leaves something to be desired, even though that 'something' was not, strictly speaking, of a technical nature.

I was about to start a lesson on doubles play for six ladies, and another qualified coach was with me for some free training. 'You play in with those three, and I'll play doubles with these three,' I suggested. I made it clear to him not to worry about poor stroke technique, but just to correct the positional and tactical aspects of their doubles play.

After the lesson, with all the ladies having gone home extremely happy with the coaching from my assistant that morning, I asked him how he felt it had gone on his court. 'Brilliant' he replied, 'they all knew what they were doing, so nothing to say, really.' Well, at least this explained why I had not heard any comments from him, and why there were no interruptions to the doubles play on his court that morning, when there were plenty on mine. But I knew the standard of my customers and had frequently glanced across to his court, and in virtually every rally, as I expected, there was at least one lady out of position. I even witnessed a volley from the baseline without any comment from my visiting assistant coach.

This example not only demonstrates inept teaching, but also how players will continue with coaching quite unaware of the poor quality of the advice they are receiving, or, as in this case, not receiving. Of course, I should have given those three ladies a refund, and an apology for that week. And here is another instance of inadequate coaching which, if you still retain your sense of humour, you might find amusing.

Quite recently, a newly-qualified coach attended an interview with a view to working at my academy. I set up a practical lesson for him with a lady who was particularly unorthodox and quite short, and asked him how he would improve her technically in the long term, on the understanding that the lady wanted to play her forehand and backhand drives, and serve, with the correct style in future. He was given twenty minutes on each stroke to assess and start correcting. All I wanted him to demonstrate to me was that he knew the fundamentals of the basic strokes.

But all I witnessed – you must be getting used to this by now – was an hour of hitting balls, with encouraging commentary, or white noise, interspersed with some humour. However, the real humour came when I asked him to summarise the lesson he had given the lady, and to leave her with one tip for each of her strokes.

'For the forehand, I suggest you bend your knees,' the coach advised; 'for your backhand, just bend your knees a little more,' he added; 'and for your serve, if you could just bend your knees a little bit, then it would be much better,' he concluded.

I cannot honestly remember how I reacted on hearing such words of wisdom, whether I actually laughed, or considered reaching for the anti-depressants: what I do know is that I just could not bring myself to give him a job. And this was a qualified coach, ready (on paper) to venture out and teach our juniors how to play, or improve at tennis.

I assure you that this was not an unusual occurrence in my time as a coach, but, rather, a sad testimony to the hugely inadequate training that takes place. It goes without saying that this coach was officially passed by the LTA as being up to at least the basic standard required to teach tennis (Level 3 in the LTA coaching structure) and, yet, with all three of the main strokes in tennis, he did not have the slightest clue as to what he was looking for. Moreover, and this is even worse, he believed he was quite competent to teach, and had just given a perfectly good lesson. To put it bluntly, such a coach should never have a hope of passing at any level, let alone Level 3.

On one of my examining days for a coaching organisation, I recall testing a rather nervous-looking coach on the double-handed backhand drive, and, feeling sorry for him, I decided to swap my hands round the wrong way as a nice and easy introduction for him on his technical fault-finding. I was surprised, to say the least, that he never fathomed out what I was doing wrong, and could not correct me.

But, when I repeated this obvious fault for the next three coaches, I was absolutely shocked that none of them spotted the problem either, and they all continued to offer me meaningless advice as I played backhand shots feeling incredibly awkward with my hands the wrong way round.

I should explain that many under-ten year-olds often get their hands mixed up when playing double-handed backhand drives, so it is important for a coach to be able to spot this problem, but none of them did. This, of course, is bad enough, but there is worse to come: all four coaches were returning to be tested for an upgrade – in other words, they were already in clubs coaching our juniors, and anyone else who came along.

I once asked an experienced coach how he went about teaching the serve. His answer was as follows: 'I just make sure my customers learn a good serving ritual, and then I find they do very well'. My response to this is: did anyone teach Nadal to adopt his long-winded serving ritual, which includes pinching his backside, or Djokovic to bounce the ball up to twenty-eight times? How does teaching like this have any bearing on learning the correct service technique?

I also hear at conferences how coaches often dislike teaching adults, as they never seem to improve. Here is an immediate admission of not understanding technique and how important it is, which is why the adult customers of such coaches do not get any better.

Technique is everything, in my opinion, as I have said at least once before. My co-author tells me it is much more than that, but I make no apologies because it is absolutely crucial and needs repeating, especially as we are dealing with tennis in Great Britain. Coming back to my argument, then, without technique you simply reduce considerably your chances of ever reaching a good standard.

When learning to play a tennis stroke, I can report that only about half the coaches I have asked know that a pupil absorbs the information being passed to him in one of three ways. So the importance of learning through the best way or means is enormous, since in some cases a player will only make progress if the coach uses the best means for that player to learn. Once I establish the best way for a pupil to learn, I tend to approach the lesson using his preferred way, and write this next to his name in my notes.

As you might anticipate, I have an example to illustrate this.

After a tennis conference in Essex, I was able to teach a coach's girlfriend to hit the ball with topspin in under ten minutes, whereas her boyfriend had failed to do so during hours and hours of coaching, spanning a whole year. There was nothing difficult about teaching this lady: it was just imperative that she was taught using the right means for her, and a means, incidentally, unknown to her boyfriend – a well-qualified coach of many years' experience.

Needless to say, I did not learn about these three different ways of learning on any coaches' course, so perhaps I should be surprised that as many as half the coaches I have chatted to about this matter are actually aware of it. It was lucky that I discovered such a vital aspect for teaching tennis early on in my career, when I happened to read about it in an American coaching magazine. If I ever had a say in devising any training for coaches, this information would certainly be very high on the agenda.

It was in 1995 that I truly became aware of the scale of the problem in British coaching, and I began to see clearly the poor expertise, and even the sheer incompetence, of so many experienced tennis coaches. Up to that time, any training I had been asked to give was usually to inexperienced coaches, so I assumed I was generally meeting those with the least knowledge.

In my first ten years as a full-time coach, I too was constantly looking for answers and, to that end, as stated already in the book, I picked the brains of other coaches from around the world, as I still had a lot to learn, but I did at least have, from day one, having learnt it through Piers Bastard, a sound understanding of all the basics, both technically and tactically, which coaches in this country just do not get taught.

But in 1995 I discovered that even our best coaches were lacking in any real expertise when a top tennis club asked me to take part in its interview process for their next coach. I was to carry out the on-court practical test for the five shortlisted candidates. All five had been county, if not international, players in their day, and had CVs many a coach dreams of possessing. One of those who did not make the shortlist had even been the captain of her country's Federation Cup team.

All of them came across almost equally impressively in their interviews. After I had carried out the on-court test with the fourth candidate, however, I nervously informed the interviewing club committee that, yet again, for the fourth time, the coach was not up to much. One of my criteria for the on-court test was: would I be prepared to send my own children to the coach for a lesson? The vague instructions being shouted down the court often had me, as well as the pupils participating, wondering what they really meant, and were not precise enough to enable beginners to learn to play properly. The coaches' knowledge was so poor on the technical side of the game that any deficiencies the pupils had in their strokes were never going to be improved.

It was even interesting to watch how bad their ball-feeding was as well, since this caused unnecessary problems for those who were trying to learn the basics.

The fifth and last coach to be interviewed at this top club, however, came from the Czech Republic. I could not believe the difference. Concise, confident and correct answers were given to my questions, and all his instructions were immediately understood and followed by the same beginners who had been somewhat confused with the previous four. The Czech Republic coach had a different system from mine, but it was perfectly logical and sound, and, unlike the other British coaches, he did at least have a system. He also knew the technical basics, which is why he made such an immediate difference to the beginners he was asked to coach.

I shall never forget the relief that I felt halfway through testing him – I would finally be able to make a recommendation to the committee. Looking back, I find it very significant and revealing that the only decent coach on view that day was the one who had learnt his trade outside the British Isles. I was glad that the club offered him the job because he was by far the best candidate.

I have to report, though, that, sadly for the club, the candidate from the Czech Republic, almost as soon as he accepted the Head Coach position, had to turn it down because of visa problems. What a loss to British tennis.

This long, one-day interviewing process really opened my eyes to the incompetence that was rife in British tennis coaching from top to bottom. Here, for the first time, I was judging coaches who were very experienced, of a high playing standard, and all in possession of the top coaching qualifications, and, yet, except for the candidate from the Czech Republic, none of them could coach properly.

It is very important to mention here that the players who were guinea pigs in the interviewing process were quite complimentary about the coaching they had received from the four British candidates, until they sampled the very different and real coaching from the man from the Czech Republic – they then realised just how much more effective a tennis lesson could be.

At this juncture, I should perhaps explain more fully my position on the teaching of tennis.

It may well be that you, the reader, question – legitimately – my approach, and you do not consider technique as that important; or you may believe that there are several acceptable techniques for a backhand drive, for example, and not just one.

It is most certainly true that I am a huge believer in technique, and the coaching of it from lesson one, in contrast to LTA-trained coaches, but, on the second point – 'several acceptable techniques' – I might well agree with you. Or, if I explain myself a little more, you might come round to my interpretation as to what is an acceptable technique.

The fact is, every top tennis player has five technical elements in common at the end of his backswing for a single-handed backhand drive: that is to say, five identifiable technical elements which every top player incorporates into the stroke. Because I have discovered this, I have naturally put it into my coaching method for the backhand drive, or backhand topspin, as it is often referred to, and therefore teach these five elements to all my students. And everyone plays a very sound backhand drive as a result.

But, and this is important for understanding the differences that people see, by incorporating the five technical elements at the end of the backswing, each player might also make other moves which are unique to that player, or they may exaggerate some of these five required elements in their backswing, so, to the untrained eye, there appear to exist different techniques, but this is not really the case.

What happens is, there are parameters within which a player must remain to be technically correct, and this means that players who incorporate the five essential technical elements can do it their way, with a longer, or shorter, backswing, for example, and therefore do not have identical backhand drives – they are, after all, human beings, and not robots. However, if anyone falls outside the parameters I have identified, then he will struggle to play the shot properly and consistently.

It is interesting that there were two top male players in recent times, both now retired, who often failed to incorporate these five elements, and, as a consequence, their backhand drives frequently let them down, and they would be the first to admit it. So, on this basis, do you not think that teaching players the backhand drive, with the five technical elements I have noticed at the end of the backswing of all top players, is a very good idea? Is it not eminently sensible to do so?

And all coaches, to whom I have explained this, think it is absolutely spot-on, and proceed to use it in their own classes. Furthermore, they all recognise that I have presented them with something that actually happens in top tennis with regard to the end of the backswing position for the backhand drive, i.e. it is not just the opinion of a quirky coach, and they all agree it is even more remarkable because they have never come across it on any of their courses.

You might be interested to know, and possibly not surprised, that the same principles apply, i.e. the 'five elements', to the forehand drive. Logically, of course, for every stroke in tennis there exist similar technical parameters which a player must not breach if he is to possess the consistency necessary for the higher levels of the sport.

Of relevance to the above, I relate the following: a few years ago, an exceptionally talented girl came to me for coaching and asked me for help with her backhand topspin. After completely reshaping it, which included teaching her the five technical elements at the end of her backswing, she asked me to write down what I was telling her to do so that she could show it to her father.

He turned up the following week and presented me with a video cassette entitled *How to play the backhand drive*. 'Could you take a look at this, please, and let me know what you think, because I cannot see anything that you have written down mentioned on this tape.'

I duly looked at the video and realised that the father was absolutely right. I had to tell him that the instructions on the tape were very poor, that much of what was said was quite frankly irrelevant, and likely to do more harm than good.

'Well, I must admit, I bought it because my daughter was struggling so much with her backhand, but it didn't seem to work, but why isn't what you've written down for me mentioned on this video?' You probably know the answer already if you have read everything, or mostly everything, so far – and have been concentrating, of course – so I do not need to go into the details of my explanation to the girl's father. Needless to say, the talented girl left with a very happy father, and a sound topspin backhand in her armoury.

However, what amazed me was how the coach on the video managed to fill forty-five minutes of tape with such meaningless and misleading advice, and actually believed he was providing good coaching. And, moreover, he was considered to be one of the very best in Great Britain, but, when I questioned him by telephone about his video, he was honest enough to admit that he did not know what all players with an excellent backhand drive do, and was impressed with the five technical elements I told him about that all top professionals have, none of which he had mentioned on his tape.

Furthermore, his video had been available for a number of years, and he informed me that I was the first person to question its content. Yet again, this is another sad, and worrying, reflection on the poor state of coaching in this country, and another clear indication of the mess we are in.

As if you needed more convincing about what really goes on, I can provide you with the following example: while visiting a top indoor centre, once considered by Judy Murray for her son Andy's junior development, I observed an advanced coaching session for eleven to fourteen year-olds. May I remind you that eleven to fourteen is a crucially important period in the development of a tennis player. Eight juniors in turn were receiving individual technical coaching for their backhand topspin drives from a highly regarded coach. But, for each junior, the coaching advice given was identical, even though six of them had different problems that needed specific, individual advice.

Every now and then, the coach would stop feeding, face the same way as the junior, and demonstrate a double-handed drive in slow motion, with the comment 'Like this'. His demonstration, or shadow stroke as we call it in tennis, of how to play the backhand topspin was superb, but none of the eight juniors changed anything in the way they played their backhand topspins, because they were not made aware of the individual technical faults they had, and how to eliminate them. The other two did have sound backhand topspin drives, and this was clearly evident from the fact that neither of them hardly missed any shots from the coach's feed, so why the coach still gave his shadow stroke reminder to these two, I really do not know.

I would venture to say, however, that the coach was simply not able to identify the soundness, or lack of soundness, in the drives of the eight juniors, so, when they missed a couple of shots, he decided his best option was to demonstrate a very good backhand drive, which he knew he possessed, and hoped that they would improve by copying.

Ideally, all the six juniors with problems should have been given a proper, one-to-one explanation of where they were going wrong, and what they then needed to do. Next, they should have been put through the right practice drill to ensure they achieved the necessary technical changes that would correct their backhand topspins.

As it was, the coaching that these advanced junior players were receiving was virtually useless. There is a saying that goes: 'If you do as you've always done, you'll get what you've always got', and it was so applicable to the situation I was witnessing.

Crucially, though, the coach should have been making a difference, and changing what the six juniors had always done, and therefore helping them to progress up the tennis ladder, but this is tennis in Great Britain, so what do you expect?

Considering that I was watching some of Britain's most serious and dedicated juniors, all of whom had been attending for over a year what was one of the seventeen High Performance Centres in the UK, all of them should by now have had really sound basics.

No wonder Carl Maes, the high-calibre and famous Belgian coach hired by the LTA, said that our fourteen year-olds were not up to scratch. If only the parents, paying lots of money for their children's intensive coaching, knew how ineffective the teaching was at one of Britain's top indoor tennis centres, then something might have changed for the better as a result of their complaints, but, of course, they would never know, because they were placing their trust, in good faith, in a fully-qualified professional who should have known what he was doing. Unfortunately, the parents would have put any lack of progress down to their children not being quite good enough, instead of the truth, which is that the coach was not quite good enough.

It goes without saying that such coaches should know better, and would know better – much better – in my opinion, after proper training. But who, at the LTA, will have the courage, the wisdom, and the energy to transform the way our coaches are trained and, in the process, transform the prospects of our juniors?

The tennis coaching tips once given on the box of a famous brand of washing powder are a clear indication of how meaningless most coaching is in the UK. Three tips were printed with the opportunity to earn a lesson with a coach in your area.

The first tip was: 'Keep your eyes on the ball', which is fatuous in the extreme, because anyone not watching the ball would never swing their racquet at it; the second was: 'Stay on your toes'; and the third: 'Keep moving your feet'. The last two tips, apart from not educating anyone particularly, since they are more or less telling a player simply to be ready, virtually amount to the same instruction.

What a waste of time and space, when three pieces of really instructive and useful coaching advice could have been given, instead of something that was just misleading and irrelevant.

This washing powder tennis promotion sums up British coaching rather neatly, in my opinion. Obviously, the person who decided upon the coaching tips did not have any better ideas, or was badly advised, not surprisingly, or, perhaps, he just did not know the first thing about tennis coaching. All very similar to Channel 4's coaching tips I mentioned in Chapter 8.

I cannot tell you how frustrated I have become hearing so many coaches over so many years give advice to players that teaches virtually nothing. The above 'Keep your eyes on the ball' is one such example; another is 'Keep your balance'. I for one, in over twenty-five years of coaching, have never ever given either instruction.

'Watch the ball' or 'Keep your eyes on it', is invariably said after the pupil has mishit a shot, but this will actually make the player worse if he literally tries to watch the ball more closely or carefully, as it will interfere with his natural flow. Putting it quite simply, everyone watches the ball on a tennis court, otherwise they would not know when to swing in order to make contact with it. And of even more interest, few players, including professionals, ever try and watch the ball when they are hitting it. And I have action stills that show this quite clearly.

And with regard to 'Keep your balance': if a player does not fall over, this basically means he must have kept his balance, so this is another worthless tip which is only given because the coach cannot honestly offer any real, constructive advice.

While occasionally a player can lose his balance when

playing a shot, this is only the result, or the effect, of something else causing him to do so. There is little need to mention it therefore. If a player loses his balance when serving for example, it is nearly always because of a poor ball toss, so the tip should be not to attempt to stretch and still serve the ball if it is incorrectly positioned when thrown in the air. Suggesting to a pupil he should keep his balance will only have him concentrating on the wrong thing: i.e. the effect (balance), and not the cause (ball toss). Most importantly, such advice will not rectify the problem.

I have no intention of turning this book or chapter into a coaching manual, so let me return to the next item on the agenda, which is a rather interesting article that appeared in a well-known tennis magazine, which I still possess, written by a top coach and former international player who stated that technique is not that important.

He reported that he had deliberately demonstrated hitting a ball successfully over the net in a way that looked both unusual and awkward, in the hope of drawing the following response, which indeed he achieved, from his adult beginners' class: 'That didn't look very good,' a lady commented. 'What was wrong with it?,' the coach asked. 'Well, I didn't think much of your style,' she replied. The coach was now able to respond with the very comment he had planned in advance to make: 'Who cares about the technique – it's where the ball ends up that matters.'

As you might guess, I most certainly do not agree with him, and support fully the lady who voiced her disapproval – she was quite right to demand a technical lesson for the following reason: it is technique which enables a player to hit the ball in consistently, so the class needed this top coach to demonstrate and explain the correct technique properly, so that they could copy it and learn to play tennis with consistency and control.

The glaring and obvious difference between the coach and his class was technique: he possessed it in abundance, so he was able to play impressively well; they did not possess it at all, and looked as awkward as the player the coach had imitated in his demonstration, so they played poorly.

In truth, it is the technique that hits the ball in, not the player. If we take Greg Rusedski, for example: in matches he struggled at times with his backhand drive, failing, on occasion, to complete all five of the essentials at the end of his backswing. When he did achieve all five technical elements, he hit magnificent backhand topspins; when he did not, he invariably missed. Here we have the same player sometimes using the right technique, and other times the wrong technique. Put simply, the right technique enabled Mr. Rusedski nearly always to hit the ball in, and the wrong technique caused him to fail. It is not the player who gets the ball in, but the...

My co-author says that, if you do not know the answer by now, you have not been paying attention – you obviously need a rest from this long chapter.

The scenario I have just described, with the ex-professional player turned coach and his class of adult beginners, is yet another sad reflection on tennis in Great Britain: I strongly suspect that the coach in question is not really sure of what or how he is supposed to teach from a technical point of view, so he plumps for the easy way out by saying that technique does not matter – emphasising that it is more about 'just doing it' and 'believing in yourself'.

I very much hope I am starting to convince you that correct technique does play an absolutely vital role in tennis, and not only at the top of the sport, but at the bottom as well.

If we in Great Britain, through our coaches, both at grass-roots level and above, do not know how to teach technically, and have no system to follow, then we are doomed forever more. As stated before in the book, there is only one basic technique for each stroke in tennis, even though different styles sometimes mask the common factors that exist for every one of them, especially when viewed at normal speed. Slow it down on a video, and that basic technique, common to all high-level players, can be identified after careful analysis.

I am well aware that many people working within the tennis industry are of the opinion that teaching technically is the wrong way to coach tennis. They will claim that, in the past, there was too much emphasis on the teaching of technique, and this stifled any natural flair and talent a player possessed.

All I can say is that the emphasis years ago may have been to coach technically, but the only reason it was not successful was because the coaches did not teach it correctly, so this would explain why the Coaching Department moved away from this.

In recent years, the 'game-based approach' has been a popular coaching system to use, but I am afraid I cannot agree with this way of teaching at all. Like the aforementioned top-down approach attempted by the LTA, it is completely the wrong way to create strong foundations for a player's tennis game. And I have read many articles written by tennis experts supporting my opinions with regard to the game-based approach: I am therefore not alone in my thinking.

I will spare you all the details of this method of learning, otherwise this chapter may never end.

It is very important, though, to make it clear that there are some coaches who do indeed see the inadequacies of the qualification courses they have attended, and, in consequence, try to put together their own coaching methods. As you may have realised, I myself have devised my own methods, which, in my opinion, and that of other coaches I have shown them to, are effective and well worth adopting.

But it is still not good enough, and it should not be left to chance like this: to have a few coaches dotted around the country coaching adequately, but differently from each other, is not, and has not been, a recipe for producing top tennis players. The solution is so easy, and all the totally inept tennis coaching that goes on now could be replaced by a simple and sound learning process, which would give many British juniors a real chance of developing into world-class players.

On 23rd October, 2010, a Daily Mail headline read: *First teacher banned for being so useless*. Another headline stated: *Bad teachers to be weeded out in Gove crackdown*. This book is about the reality of British tennis, and I am afraid the truth is that, like bad teachers, there are bound to be bad coaches who may need 'to be weeded out'. But, whereas we know about bad teachers, we shall not know who the bad tennis coaches are until they have had proper training.

If we are to have anything like the professional set-up of golf, for example, there has to be rigorous training of new coaches, and retraining for those currently employed, with exams that demand a precise understanding of the systems and methods taught on the courses. If a candidate does badly in the exam, then he fails, and cannot become a coach, or continue to be one, until he passes – as simple as that.

It has to be recognised, however, that being a good tennis coach is not that easy, just as being a good schoolteacher is not easy, either. There are many qualities which you have to learn, if not possess quite naturally in the first place, to do the job properly. Coaches have to be good with people, and know how to welcome and handle adults, juniors and younger children. They have to be organised, punctual, ultra-reliable and able to assess correctly so many different and unexpected situations. They must keep the coaching session moving, giving time to the class as a whole, and to each student individually. Everybody must be able to hear and understand what is said at all times during the lesson; there should be variety, encouragement, and some humour; and everything must take place in an environment that is absolutely safe.

I could include many more aspects, and even crib from an LTA list of thirty-five qualities I was given once while training, but I merely wish to point out that there is quite a skill to coaching, and to coaching groups in particular, and this is without covering the enormous task of the actual coaching itself, involving, ideally, a method and a system that the coach must implement and understand thoroughly. It is very much like being a schoolteacher, with pupils to handle, a subject to teach, and a syllabus to follow – all requiring considerable knowledge, sensitivity and skill.

The tragedy for British tennis is that there are undoubtedly coaches out there who are absolutely right for the job: even outdoors, on a cold winter's evening, they can deliver a lesson to juniors that has pace and enjoyment, never flags for one moment, and the atmosphere created is superb. The problem is – and it is a huge problem – that much too often there is no actual coaching taking place, and no one actually improves. There is no teaching of the technique required for the strokes of the sport, and, remember, there are more than twenty, and no correction of the faults that are inevitably on view.

Some coaches will describe themselves as 'expert skill developers', because this is the catchphrase they have learnt on their courses, but, when you see what is actually happening, or, rather, not happening, as I have for far too long now, you realise that all the passion, enthusiasm and flair they may have for their job count for virtually nothing. If only they could have been trained better to teach what really matters. What they do at present looks good and sounds good, but it does not stand up to analysis. (I think I have said this before somewhere.) For the gifted coaches who appear to give good lessons, it is usually very much a question of style over substance – not exactly the right formula if you want to make it, or want your pupils to make it, in professional sport.

As you have probably deduced by now, I am, and have been, so fed up with the situation that I was moved to write a book in protest about it – no easy thing for a non-academic like me. My co-author could not agree more – obviously thinking of all the work he has had to do to bring my writing, hopefully, up to scratch.

I very much hope that not only the mess we are in is clear by now, but that the solution is also becoming much more obvious. We are, in effect, about to move away from the main part of the book, which has been all about explaining the mess, and on to the equally important second part, which is how to get out of it.

If I may end the chapter as I started it, if you can remember that far back, with a very stark quotation from the 2006 Blueprint: 'Coaches lack credibility'. Roger Draper and his team certainly got some things right – unfortunately, actions did not speak louder than the printed word in this case, and in other cases too, one hastens to add.

I invite you to read on, for the end is nigh...

CHAPTER 12

The Solution

True to my word, the end is indeed nigh, with only this chapter and one other to go, and the good news is that neither of them is anywhere near as long as that on 'Coaching'. They do, however, form a very important part of the book and, I hope, bring it to a logical and convincing conclusion.

By now, you are probably very well aware of the way I think, and can anticipate the two parts of 'The Solution' that I am about to give. But, before I go into details, I would like to report to you the reaction of my co-author a month or so after he had agreed to help me with the onerous task, for me, of writing a book. Being an ex-LTA-qualified tennis coach, and also being far more educated and academic than I am, he not only started to give my manuscript the polish and style it was sadly lacking, but, in addition, he carried out a lot of extra research. He very soon concluded that the 'mess' of the title might have to be changed into something stronger, and wondered how, among other things, any budding LTA coach could learn to teach well, considering the content of the courses available. He supposed that the younger ones just accepted it all in order to get the right piece of paper, and the older ones took lots of Prozac – he does have a wicked sense of humour. In no way, he said, could he feel inspired by it all – on the contrary, he felt quite depressed. Despite this, he himself has not yet resorted to anti-depressants, but, then, he is an ex-schoolteacher and has great inner strength.

Part one of the solution for getting out of the mess we have in British tennis is very straightforward: much, much better training for coaches. It is simply no good the LTA churning out coaches and assistants by the bucket load, specialising in this, that, and the other, and helping to 'grow the game' in every nook and cranny, if they – the coaches and the assistants – do not come away with sufficient knowledge to teach effectively at basic grass-roots level and other levels too. By 'teach effectively', I mean teach their charges how to get the ball over the net with sound technique. Quality is far more important than quantity if we are to buck the trend of the last forty years. The training I am proposing would deliver, I believe, the quality that is necessary.

I should make it quite clear from the outset that I am completely open to being grilled about my proposals, and to discussing them fully with experts appointed by the LTA, Sport England, the Tennis Foundation, and representatives of any other sporting body. As has been done very successfully in British rugby and cycling, the questioning of everything would be most welcome and appropriate, with no sacred cows – just honesty, and an acute sense of reality.

As already stated in other parts of this book, over the years I have had many juniors, with or without parents in attendance, and adult beginners, coming to me for lessons and being amazed and thankful, at how quickly they learn and make progress, compared to what they have experienced elsewhere.

If my ideas for better training courses were accepted wholly, or in part, it would not be a question of a Brad Gilbert-like 'upskilling' of coaches, as the LTA described it in the heyday of Roger Draper (circa 2008), but, rather, it would be far more mundane, and would consist of a thorough grounding in the basics necessary for the learning of sound technique by those at grass-roots and mini tennis level.

'Swing low to high', remembered by my co-author when he qualified around 1980, and 'well-organised shapes', 'long swing planes', 'contact points' etc., all referred to in current LTA Training Programmes, are not wrong as guidelines, but, and I discovered this a long time ago in my own coaching, they are nowhere near precise enough for effective teaching. Much more detail is needed for coaching a beginner if he is to understand quickly and efficiently how to hit a ball like a proper tennis player. Sadly, such detail, which is absolutely crucial, is at present missing in the LTA courses attended by our coaches.

In the training that I have in mind, the nuts and bolts of each stroke would be laid bare so that coaches would know exactly what they had to do in their lessons, and they would therefore be far better teachers for it. If they asked me how best to do something, I would give them a straight and clear answer – after all, that is what people deserve when they want to learn. Incidentally, working for years at grass-roots level has given me an uncanny ability always to nail my colours confidently to the mast, with no hesitation whatsoever.

Coaches would also be shown that it is quite feasible to teach valuable tennis techniques to the very youngest of learners, known as 'tots' – even a full-blooded forehand drive is possible at the age of three or four.

Fun, of course, would be incorporated into lessons as appropriate to age, and even the mood of the player(s) at a given moment in time, as would some 'ABC' – i.e. agility, balance and coordination – exercises, again, as appropriate, but the overriding ethos would be the teaching of tennis and its techniques in a structured way, from the very first time someone stepped on to a tennis court with the hope of learning how to play, and it would continue in every session thereafter, ensuring logical progress and an acquisition of the skills necessary to become a complete tennis player in terms of technique.

As a result, in mini tennis programmes parents would clearly see that their children were learning, and making progress in, all the main strokes of the game – no longer would they feel the need, perhaps, to look for a better Performance Centre, or a better coach; and, when it came to adult beginners, the reaction would be equally positive on seeing how successful they were at learning to control a lively, yellow ball in a short space of time.

It would be a case of 'play and stay' all round – not because of fun, but because of genuine progress, and the resulting excitement and satisfaction of being able to play and feel like a proper tennis player. The knock-on effect of really good coaching would also be seen in the parks programmes that the LTA have been rolling out with the aim of boosting the numbers playing.

People will stay in the sport for far longer if they learn to play properly – their enjoyment will be that much greater and this, in turn, will mean that their offspring will be inspired to play the game as well, thus creating 'tennis families', in the true sense of the expression.

In addition, the numbers competing will go up, since more juniors will want to enter tournaments because they will have the true ability to control the ball through technique, and consequently feel, and know they are playing tennis properly. And can you imagine what this does for a player's confidence? Is there anything more uplifting for a young tennis player?

To tighten things up further, coaches would learn about the importance of making notes on their pupils like true professionals, and also like true professionals, at the end of the course, they would have to show a thorough understanding in an exam of what they had learnt in order to obtain the qualification certificate. Moreover, if they did not show sufficient understanding, they would not pass the exam and would, therefore, not be allowed to coach. However, with further training and practice, they would be given the chance, with the right application, to reach the required standard, as happens in other professions.

There would be a specially designated website containing extra support and relevant information on coaching; there would also be the phone number of a helpline so that advice and guidance could be immediately available, if required.

In addition, a tutor for each region would visit coaches at their bases to offer more advice and extra on-site training.

With a clear system and method to work to, I am sure that the 'coaches lack credibility' comment in the 2006 Blueprint would no longer be applicable, and, more importantly, it would cease to be voiced as an opinion by anyone connected with British tennis, i.e. the 'stakeholders', as the LTA call them.

The practicality of what I am proposing, and I emphasise that everything I say in this chapter is open to thorough discussion and analysis, would be that those wanting to enter the profession at Level 3 would pay for the new qualification course, and existing coaches would ideally not be required to do so, or would, at least, be heavily subsidised, since they would have already had to contribute to most, or all, of the costs of their original qualification courses.

The requalifying I envisage could replace that year's accreditation courses, either wholly, or in part, which coaches have to attend to retain their licence, perhaps six credits, or more, for completing the new course.

In June, 2013, Roger Draper, the outgoing Chief Executive of the LTA, said that he regretted not looking more closely at coaching in Great Britain: I firmly believe that, had he done so, he would have clearly seen that there was a desperate need to improve things, and might well have embarked on a course of action to turn the situation around. Perhaps this book would not even have been necessary – oh, what joy for me and my co-author.

As it is, I can only say that I have seen excellent results in my own coaching, albeit on a small scale, by using the system and methods I have developed; I have also had a most positive, even delighted, response from some fifty coaches who have come to me to find out about my modus operandi; I received praise for my ideas from Richard Schonborn, for twenty-six years the Head Coach of the German Tennis Federation, and voted Europe's number one coaching guru at the time that I met him in the USA; I also refer you to my co-author's comments about me at the beginning of the book. I truly believe that I have developed further the coaching ideas of the PTR, the RPT, and the LTA, and have turned them into a much more effective way of teaching tennis. I am selling myself here on the advice of my co-author, just as I did in Chapter 1. Normally, my natural English modesty prevails.

I am convinced that, with systematic, nitty-gritty teaching of technique from the start, our juniors, and other beginners, would develop much more quickly than they do now into very proficient, all-round tennis players.

There is no harm, of course, in youngsters having some fun competing in the mini red, orange and green tournaments, as happens now, but, strictly speaking, this is not absolutely essential for their early development.

In my opinion, the sooner you master the techniques of tennis, the sooner your natural talent can come to the fore in the right way, i.e. from a sound base, and turn you into a special and unique player, with no obvious weaknesses. Only then can tactical awareness and proficiency truly blossom.

For all this to happen, however, coaches must have a logical system and a very precise method of teaching: whether it is my system and my methods is open to debate, of course, but what is crucial is that there simply has to be a system in place, with the methods to go with it, because, at present, everything is far too haphazard, complicated and messy. Quite frankly, coaches are left unimpressed with their training, are forced to work things out for themselves, and all end up reaching different conclusions. This is a thoroughly unsatisfactory situation for anyone in Great Britain wanting to learn to teach properly, or wanting to learn to play properly.

With much tighter and more structured technical training, I firmly believe that the fine and imaginative words of the 2006 Blueprint would at last become reality. Just to remind you, these are they: 'In the community we will ensure that we have enough of the right coaches working in our schools and parks – coaches who have the talent to get players of all ages up, rallying and enjoying the game, fast! They will become the pied pipers of tennis'.

However, with what I am proposing, there would be a difference to, and an improvement on, the vision of 2006: the right training would ensure that all coaches, wherever they worked at grass-roots level, would not only 'get players...up, rallying and enjoying the game, fast!', but also, through sound teaching, would get them looking like proper tennis players. What an inspiring spectacle that would be!

So much for part one of the solution. Now for part two, which is equally important, bearing in mind the shenanigans described in Chapter 10 'The Coach'. Once again, may I remind you of a relevant quote from the 2006 Blueprint: 'In clubs, we will support the professionalisation of the coach, as in golf, making sure there are proper, robust coach/club contracts in place'. Reality, unfortunately, tells a different tale.

While it is true that some big clubs and commercial centres do offer their own individual contracts to coaches, it is by no means common practice for smaller clubs and bases to do so. What I am proposing is a standard, three-way, binding contract for all coaches, all over the country, no matter what sort of tennis base or bases they work at – commercial indoor centre, club, school, park, etc. By three-way, I mean that it would be a contract between the coach, the base and the LTA.

A ready-made LTA/Coach/Base skeleton contract would be on the LTA website that could be printed off by a coach or a base manager. An LTA Coach Contract Committee, set up for each region, would be available to advise on the finer details when it came to the filling in of the contract by the coach and base concerned: examples would be provided to follow as guidelines. It would then be signed by the coach and his base.

Should problems or disputes arise between the coach and his base which cannot be resolved, a Central Coach Contract Committee would arbitrate between the two parties, both of whom would be able to get in touch easily with the Contract Committee. It would, of course, work both ways, with the coach's viewpoint sometimes upheld, and, at other times, the decision would go in favour of the base. Whatever the ruling, the Contract Committee would be there to deal with the aftermath as well.

It goes without saying that the drawing up of the skeleton contract, and all the legal implications, would have to be carefully worked out by lawyers appointed by the LTA – certainly not a task for me. I only know about tennis coaching.

As with part one of 'The Solution', a special helpline would also be set up, this time to deal with contract enquiries and, if necessary, to arrange a visit by an adviser to the coach's base if there were problems. If it became obvious from numerous phone calls, or advisers' visits, that one particular problem was frequently occurring in different parts of the country, a suitable accreditation course could be put together to help deal with it, if such a course did not exist already, and coaches could be required, requested or advised to attend it.

It is worth pointing out that my co-author and I know of many coaches, both full- and part-time, who would very much appreciate such a helpline now, so that any problems they had, of whatever nature, could be discussed, and perhaps sorted out. As things are at present, a good number of coaches feel isolated, and are quite often in need of the instant answers a helpline would provide.

With the arrangement I am proposing, and, remember, a coaches' union, in the proper sense of the word, no longer exists, all qualified teachers of tennis would be so much better protected than they are now. No more dismissals on the whim of a club chairperson, etc. – I refer you to Chapter 10 'The Coach' for many examples of really appalling practices. Equally important, the behaviour of every coach would have to be thoroughly professional at all times as well – excellent punctuality, reliability, first-class preparation of lessons, and so on.

My proposal would also go a long way to regulating the tennis coaching industry, for the good of all concerned: no longer would it be possible for certain bases, as happens with some very well-known indoor centres, to employ cheaper, unregistered and unlicensed coaches with doubtful qualifications. Of course, the implications of such a lack of professionalism are quite shocking: not only does one have seriously to question the quality of the coaching provided, but recognise that there are other issues too, such as Health and Safety, public liability insurance, and the suitability of the coaches to work with children and vulnerable adults – i.e. have proper Disclosure and Barring Service (DBS) checks been carried out? etc.

As I have argued in this book, British tennis is in a mess – a mess that stems principally from poor coaching and poor training, and also the questionable treatment of coaches.

I believe that it is quite possible to get out of it by implementing the two measures I have described in this chapter. Moreover, they would not be expensive or difficult to put into practice, after, of course, due discussion, analysis, and probably some modifications.

With the security afforded by part two of the solution, and the clear, uncomplicated structure for the teaching of tennis provided by part one, a full-time career in coaching would soon become much more attractive and satisfying. In short, coaching would be transformed into a true profession, carried out by real professionals. As a result, the whole climate of tennis in Great Britain would also be transformed, and standards all round would rise, along with participation numbers too, leading finally to the success we have craved for decades.

I now invite you to read the very last chapter for my 'Final Thoughts'.

CHAPTER 13

Final Thoughts

You may well question why I went to the enormous trouble and expense, of actually writing a book about the problems in British tennis: after all, I could easily have requested a meeting with the powers that be in order to present my ideas to them. And I am sure I would have been given at least a polite hearing.

However, I should remind you that, over the years, I have tried to give my thoughts to the Governing Body of British tennis, but to no avail: when all is said and done, I am just a lowly grass-roots coach working in a park in Kent. In competition with the opinions of other people, including those of many coaches, my voice has never been sufficiently loud. I am neither famous enough, nor important enough.

In addition, there is no way that I could do justice to what is written in these pages by just having an interview with a high-ranking LTA official, or even with the man at the very top; nor could I begin to explain adequately the mess that exists in British tennis in the short space of time that would be afforded to me. The full, multifaceted picture simply had to be presented in the form of a book.

No sound bite, or series of sound bites, would have been sufficient to cover: a proper explanation of my position on the outside looking in, and how I arrived at my viewpoint; the background to the mess – the constant changes over the decades and the millions wasted on schemes which were supposed to ensure that our juniors fulfilled their potential; references to the Blueprint or Action Plan, for 2006-2016; the disconnect with reality; the flawed approach to introducing tennis into schools; the bad experiences to be had at the start of a youngster's competitive career; the misleading and thoroughly unhelpful advice on technique from TV pundits...

And, most importantly, the spoken word could never convey the magnitude of the mess as exemplified in the chapters 'The Coach' and 'Coaching': the appalling treatment meted out to many of those who try to teach tennis for a living, with no protection, support or redress, and the thoroughly inadequate training, giving rise to practices that leave so much to be desired, and leave so much for coaches to work out for themselves – that is, if they have the nous to do so, inevitably with varying degrees of success – and do not decide simply to walk away from the profession, or just plump for making the best of a bad job, and muddle through until they are able to retire.

Unfortunately, and tragically, the upshot of all this is the following: it takes a very special junior indeed to get to the top if he is guided and developed within these shores alone. And in order to convince people of this fact, a book, and not an interview or a sound bite, had to be the most appropriate means of delivery.

In the heyday of John McEnroe, a very well-known British coach published a book on tennis, and in it there was a photo of the famous American just starting his service action. The caption underneath referred to his unorthodox technique, adding that this often happens with world-class players. I would counter this by saying that Mr. McEnroe's service has the same technical elements of anyone who knows how to serve properly – it is, in fact, quite orthodox. The only unusual aspect is the way he starts, with the placing of his feet causing him to have to rotate his upper body a little more before delivering his serve. It is interesting that the coach in question delivered, in his time, literally hundreds of LTA qualification courses.

In the 1980s, having reached county standard with no formal tuition, I decided to seek help from a number of top LTA coaches because I wanted to hit my backhand drive with more topspin, and not one of them could put me right. However, in 1985, when I attended a USPTR coaches' qualification course, I had my backhand topspin corrected by the tutor, Piers Bastard, who could see my problem even before I thought of asking him. The advice I received was absolutely spot-on and, for the first time, I realised why this shot had been so inconsistent during my playing days.

As already stated in the book, having learnt nothing of value on my first qualification course run by the LTA, I had to go elsewhere in order to gain the knowledge and confidence necessary for basic, grass-roots coaching – hence, the above-mentioned encounter with Piers Bastard.

Fast-forward to 2013, and the young, fully licensed Head Coach at a big 'clubmarked' club I happen to be visiting in the south of England is taking a group of juniors for the second half of an eight-day course. The coach is fresh from the latest LTA training, and yet he does not know what his assistant has covered in the first four days; he has no notes to guide him; there are orange and yellow balls mixed up on the court; he says he is 'growing the game' and 'developing the juniors' skills', but is unable to enter into any specific details of what he has taught his class, nor can he explain to me how exactly he is 'developing their skills'. There is no method or structure on view, and I come away from it all feeling singularly uninspired, and somewhat depressed, as I realise that these poor juniors, on the eighth day of their course, do not know any more about playing tennis than when they turned up on the first day!

And if this is typical of coaching on a proper tennis court today, then the latest guidance on how to conduct a coaching session in confined spaces, given via a DVD on the LTA website, is equally uninspiring and depressing in all its shocking inadequacy.

As for the years in between, I have reported on a newly-qualified young coach who was not provided with one single technical tip on how to teach the serve, and I have also referred to one of the leading coaches in the country at the time, who came up with quite fatuous comments in an instructional video regarding the two most common faults displayed by the average recreational player when hitting a forehand drive.

But if that is not bad enough, may I remind you of the coach in one particular county, holding the highest possible qualifications, who only ever sang to his juniors during lessons.

From a coaching perspective, can it get any worse, or more desperate, than this?

It sometimes seems to me that the ball boys and girls at Wimbledon receive better training than our junior tennis players do, or anyone else trying to learn, for that matter. For the ball kids, the instructions are so precise –

they are told: how to hold the balls; the grip changes to make according to what they have to do with the balls; how to move; how to throw or pass the balls; their exact position on court according to what they are doing; how to anticipate and react to unusual situations... The result is that they do an excellent job, derive great satisfaction from it, and even have fun at the same time. Of course, with slapdash training, the epithet 'excellent' would go out of the window, and any enjoyment would soon evaporate in the face of protests from the players and public alike.

If you are young, or not so young, and have serious intentions of learning to play properly, how can you achieve your goals in the climate that prevails in the UK? Any coaching tips from the television or radio are frankly misleading and ill-informed, and the ethos on mini, Cardio and 'Tennis Xpress' courses, all with low compression balls, is very much about FUN, and see how easy it is.

Certainly, the ITF (International Tennis Federation) are fully behind the concept of 'Play and stay' – make it fun and make it easy – because they want to increase participation in the sport globally, and it is a way of getting people on to a tennis court. But, whether you are into mini tennis, Cardio tennis with music, for fitness, or 'Tennis Xpress', where you learn the rudiments of the game, you still have the problem of eventually having to learn how to play with normal and very lively yellow balls: with low-compression ones, you can take liberties and get away with murder in the technical sense, and still keep a rally going. But, in order to play tennis properly, you simply have to have good coaching so that you learn the different techniques for the strokes, otherwise your experience of proper tennis with lively balls will be frustrating and off-putting.

Fun will be very short-lived therefore, which explains

why numbers on courts quickly decline, unless many more initiatives can be invented and undertaken by the LTA to attract the next batch of unsuspecting punters.

For our juniors in the mini tennis situation, especially the more serious ones who want to learn, there is not just the problem of fun getting in the way, but also the rules about different colour low-compression balls for different age groups.

Much criticism is often heard from both coaches and parents regarding how rigid and complicated it all is when trying to effect a change of ball colour for a talented youngster who is ready to move up, but is not officially old enough. Indeed, the whole competitive structure for six to ten year-olds is frequently described as being so highly regulated that one's sanity can feel threatened when dealing with it.

No wonder Martin Baldridge, the author of *So You Want to Win Wimbledon?: How to Turn the Dream Into Reality*, has said that the LTA have micromanaged the game into recession.

Judy Murray has stated, and many would agree with her, that, by the time a youngster is eleven or twelve, he should not only have all the basic strokes of the game, but also variety. Unfortunately for British tennis, if you visit High Performance Centres, or look in on regional training camps, you will see technical deficiencies that should have been sorted out long ago.

It is an indictment of British coaching that I have had juniors come to my academy in the park and be so relieved, and grateful, to receive actual coaching, rather than the fun that had been served up to them elsewhere: all they wanted was to learn how to get the ball over the net consistently and effectively.

Before Easter each year, I used to be fully booked until December, with just the holiday courses to fill, but these too were always oversubscribed, needing only minimal advertising.

The youngsters 'played and stayed' because they were learning and making progress. As a result, I coached and 'stayed' in the profession, otherwise I simply could not have put up with scratching around for work, or trying to teach in the haphazard and unstructured way that has been so heavily criticised in this book.

From a professional standpoint, it was a crying shame that, prior to setting up my own academy, I was rarely at a base where I was able to encourage serious juniors to attend my programmes more than twice a week, when they really needed so much more, but this, sadly, was and is, the reality for a good number of full-time tennis coaches in Great Britain, especially those not fortunate enough to work at a really big club. In my own case, I simply had to make sure I worked at several bases, with large numbers of customers attending my programmes just once a week, in order to give myself some security and a chance to survive. In this way I managed to avoid the highly undesirable situation of many other coaches who simply could not stay afloat.

I felt, and still feel, great satisfaction from having given many youngsters a skill for life, even though some were not talented enough to make it, or to be fair to many of them, tennis was not their number one priority. At least, they learnt to play like proper tennis players, and not like beginners.

FUN as a priority in coaching, i.e. teaching, is a travesty, of course. It is interesting that the LTA, having been 'put on notice' by Sport England for failing to increase the numbers playing tennis in the UK, are still considered to be in 'special measures' by the same body – terminology used by Ofsted when dealing with schools and education. Tennis coaching has to be about educating people in the sport, otherwise what possible purpose can it have? As is well-known, there is no inspection regime for coaches in this country – but, then, what sensible criteria could be used for the amount of FUN in a lesson? With a proper system and method in place, as proposed in Chapter 12 'The Solution', there would at least be something to inspect.

It is supremely ironic that the comedian and tennis player, Tony Hawks, was in serious conflict with the LTA some ten years ago about taking tennis to the masses and getting into the parks. The response at the time was so negative that he and a business partner had virtually to set it all up on their own in the form of TFF (Tennis For Free), persuading local boroughs not to charge for their park courts, and organising free or very cheap coaching. Now, and here is the irony, the LTA are inundating the parks, and other places, with promotional campaigns, offering free this and free that, spending millions, telling all and sundry that tennis is not expensive. You can even, apparently, hire balls if need be when playing with friends, and it is all accompanied, as one would expect, by lots of press releases and marketing.

A complete sea change, compared to a few years ago.

But this is what the LTA have done for decades, going from one scheme to another, and, when one does not deliver, it is binned and something else is tried. This time, however, almost everybody is saying that this is what needs to be done to turn British tennis around: not top-down any more, but start at the bottom – i.e. get the grass roots right.

There is absolutely nothing wrong, of course, with being inclusive, creating loads of 'places to play' and increasing the participation numbers, but it is not a panacea – quantity is not quality.

At a top club, a senior figure in British tennis enthused about one of the mini tennis courts on view, saying that twenty-five youngsters could get on it all at once, and their parents could also learn to play by enrolling on a 'Tennis Xpress' course at the same club. Whole families whacking low-compression balls and having fun.

But what about some first-class coaching and a bit of common sense being applied to the idea of twenty-five juniors on the same mini tennis court?

It is interesting that golf does not have to resort to such frantic measures in order to persuade people to take up the sport. It is also interesting to consider the answer that the Irish ex-pro golfer and broadcaster, Maureen Madill, gave in 2013 when she was asked about how it was that so many ladies from the Far East were now dominating the world at golf: 'Well, if you introduce lots of young girls into the sport and throw a load of money in their direction, how can you fail?' And of course she was right – how can you fail? If the right guidance is there, you obviously cannot fail.

In Great Britain, however, unlike in other sports where juniors do come through, we have thrown loads of money in the direction of our tennis youngsters for decades, but the simple truth is that the right guidance has never been there, and, as I complete this book, is still not there, apart from that given by a handful of coaches dotted around the country, who have individually, and in isolation, worked out how to teach the fundamentals of tennis. But they will also report how they usually lose their protégés into a system which then fails these potential star players.

It is perhaps relevant here to ask why the LTA have never become aware of the deficiencies in their Coaching Department: after all, they regularly ask people in tennis for their opinions about what needs to be addressed in order to put matters right. They also have the resources and, in particular, the money, to correct just about anything they want.

I, for one, though, can quite understand why the message has never got through. If the coaches themselves are asked for their opinions, they are hardly going to rock the boat, like me, and be highly critical of their training: it is simply not in their interest to do so if they want to make a career out of coaching. And this is assuming that they have the necessary criteria to be critical – many will probably go on courses and simply accept what they are given, thinking that it is the norm. In addition, a good number of them will have only just finished being on the receiving end as juniors themselves, and not have anything else with which to compare their training. In other words, they do not know any different.

And the image projected by the Coaching Department to the outside world, and within the LTA, is a most positive one: a multitude of qualification courses are on offer that produce coaches and assistants in their droves; for the 'Performance' side the coaches appear eminently suitable because of their high playing standard; the dazzling array of extra accreditation courses (Continuous Professional Development) seem to cover every aspect of tennis under the sun, and therefore appear to be comprehensive and thorough; and it is all marketed most impressively with glossy brochures and wonderful descriptions of 'cutting edge' training that almost take one's breath away.

However, the reality is something else entirely, as has been amply shown in this book.

'All I want to do, from the very first lesson, is learn how to get the ball over the net in a way that is not dissimilar to what a professional does, and I want to do it time and time again, otherwise there is no fun or enjoyment in playing because I'll be spending more time picking up the balls than actually trying to win points in a game.'

These are the typical sentiments of those just starting out at grass-roots level. Unfortunately, what they want and need, whether they are young or not so young, is simply not there because the basic core is missing in the training given to our coaches. Ironically, everything else is there, except, unbelievably in my view, the down-to-earth, nitty-gritty advice on how to play the different shots in all their fascinating detail.

As confirmation of all this from my own experience, I have written a manual on how to conduct a group lesson and teach the most important strokes of the game – all very basic and practical – but none of the key points has ever been covered in a course I have been on; for coaches wanting to work at my academy, some of whom had been teaching for years, I had a simple questionnaire on the very common problems that arise at grass-roots level, but no one ever managed to get more than a quarter of the answers right; and the fifty or so coaches who have come to me for training reveal such a lack of knowledge of how to go about teaching the basics of the game that it is both frightening and depressing at the same time. The only positive and pleasing aspect being that they go away grateful for what they have learnt.

One of the measures of success of any tennis federation is the number of players in the singles top 100: the record of the LTA is, and has been, abysmal. There has never been a production line of players coming through, as is the case with countries like Spain, France, Italy, Germany, Russia, Argentina, some Eastern European countries, and so on...

Not very long ago, there were half a dozen German men in the first round of a Grand Slam, and they all lost, giving rise to great disquiet and considerable Teutonic angst. If we had experienced the same situation, or had even had six men in the last round of qualifying, our reaction would have been positive in the extreme – at last, we were getting somewhere, we would have triumphantly concluded.

At the time of writing, we are in the World Group of the Davis Cup, but, remember, you only need one outstanding singles player and one doubles specialist to partner him in order to achieve success. In our case, unfortunately, independence for Scotland would immediately put paid to any hopes of reaching the heights in the said competition, and the women would probably lose Judy Murray as the captain of the Federation Cup team as well.

It is a sad fact that in Great Britain you have to be a genius, or outrageously talented, to come through – Virginia Wade, Sue Barker, Tim Henman, Andy Murray – and usually with the help of tennis-connected parents and some wealth within the family.

The merely talented players will make it to county level, and then stop. It is my contention that, with better coaching from scratch, some of these players would go beyond county standard and start to become part of the production line mentioned above.

When someone like Tim Henman very occasionally makes it, the LTA usually claim responsibility, or some responsibility, for the success. The truth is, however, there will always be exceptions, and some, with a lot of talent and a lot of drive, will come through despite the system. If the training regimes were sound, many more players would be appearing on a regular basis, year after year, as happens in other countries.

'Do not stay here – go abroad', usually to America, was the advice given to the parents of young tennis players with high hopes some thirty-plus years ago. Unfortunately, nothing much has changed since then: Andy Murray (Spain), Heather Watson (Florida)... It is not surprising that players on the WTA and ATP tours consider Great Britain to be a weak tennis nation; and Nick Bollettieri, the famous Florida coach, said in 2013 that we in Britain just do not 'do' pro tennis players.

It does not have to be like this, of course: with the right system, 'Stay here' would be the automatic response to any request for advice about what to do. It would also be a much less expensive option and open up possibilities for literally anyone, no matter what their background. In addition, unlike in other countries, financial help in the form of LTA 'matrix' funding for the really talented and deserving is on offer, together with quality individual guidance.

'Tennis is in a good place in Great Britain' is a phrase that the LTA have started to use since Andy Murray won Wimbledon in July, 2013, and it seems that the British public, and those who work in the media, are more than ready to accept it. On Sky Sports, in March, 2013, Andrew Castle, Barry Cowan, Peter Fleming, and Mark Petchey all agreed that British tennis was in a bad way. So what has changed? When the four commentators gave their judgement, Andy Murray was already a Grand Slam champion. Now he has added the greatest Grand Slam title of all to his name, but the reality is still there.

Have we all gone gooey-eyed simply because the

remarkable Scotsman has won Wimbledon? Or is it that, true to our national character, we are too polite and reserved to criticise because there is a new Chief Executive Officer from Canada at the helm and we are waiting to see how he gets on? Perhaps it is a combination of the two, but, whatever the case, if you are reading this book, rose-tinted glasses and an excess of politeness have never been part of the agenda, although I do wish Mr. Downey well, of course – his job is key, and most certainly demanding.

I am just a grass-roots coach and reality is all I know. I am not famous, and I have put my head above the parapet. I have done what others have told me they would also like to do, but desist because they are fearful of the consequences. I may well be shot down, but, at least, I have tried. My desire is simply to improve the state of British tennis, which I have observed and experienced from outside the LTA system for over twenty-five years.

There are so many good things already in place for high-level players, but, first, they have to reach that high level, and not nearly enough are doing so. It could all be much, much better, especially in the early years at the grass roots and just above, where it really matters.

At present, if you are a good tennis player and do not know much else, you can easily become a coach and earn way above the legal minimum hourly rate set by the government; you can also become one of the many who are carrying out the LTA strategy of 'growing the game'. It is very much a case of all hands to the pump and get as many as possible having fun on a tennis court. But where is the wisdom in all of this?

In accordance with the proposals put forward in the last chapter 'The Solution', all coaches, whether Level

3, 'Performance' or otherwise, would know the basics of teaching tennis from scratch – i.e. the nuts and bolts of each stroke – so that beginners of any age could start to learn quickly and efficiently to control the ball with sound technique. They would engage with young, and not so young, people by teaching and helping them to make solid, and exciting progress.

My vision is simply for all coaches to be equipped to do a truly professional job every time they give a lesson, and for all, without exception, to have a proper contract that protects them and their base, whether they teach on a humble park court, or in the poshest of indoor centres. There would no longer be unregistered coaches plying their doubtful trade in unsuspecting, or not so unsuspecting, clubs, or in settings beyond the reach of the LTA and any talent identification.

They would be like schoolteachers with a syllabus to follow and ways to deliver it – in short, they would have a system and a method to work to. Clarity, simplicity and structure would prevail, in contrast to the haphazard, over-complicated and random mess that exists now.

In my own coaching I have found that beginners of any age and any ability, are not put off at all by proper teaching – on the contrary, they respond with great enthusiasm, and come back again and again. After all, what do you want to learn when you first venture on to a tennis court? It has to be: how to get the ball over the net in a way that is not dissimilar to what you see in a professional tennis match.

A coach cannot teach people to have Andy Murray's will to win, but he should be able to teach the way he hits the ball.

The outstanding Scotsman has said that there are some great people in British tennis, but they do not talk to each other. Well, let us start talking. I, for one, am happy to do so.

It would be wonderful to hear an LTA representative on Sky Sports, for example, explaining how talent identification and the matrix system for funding players work, especially since there has been criticism that it is all too complicated. It would also be very refreshing if such a representative were more than willing to discuss other aspects of tennis in the UK.

From my own perspective, i.e. the grass roots, we simply cannot continue to let the keenest of our youngsters down, or anyone else, for that matter. The stark truth is, if a junior is talented and serious, and does not get what he wants out of his tennis lessons, he will be off trying another sport, never to return.

The solution, though, is remarkably simple, and quite basic.

But before I finish, I have to emphasise that I have written this book because, above all, I care.

I care about British tennis, I care about the coaches out there who are trying to make an honest living, and I care about the children who attend coaching, wishing either to learn to play properly, or go further and pursue tennis as a career with the intention of possibly turning professional .

I hope that the LTA care as well, I am sure they do, and are even grateful that someone, coming from the grass roots and with a certain amount of expertise, has flagged up the reality that has existed for at least the last thirty years, and still exists, and is able to offer a solution to a problem that has seemed so intractable.

They can criticise, or they can consult, or go for a combination of the two, but, at least, let there be a reaction.

If you want to get in touch with me:
http://www.stevekitchertennisacademy.com

About the Author

Having coached tennis for over 25 years, Steve has recently semi-retired, giving him the time to enjoy his other interests, golf and the classical guitar, as well as importantly completing this book - an ambition of his for 15 years.

Despite being a sports fanatic and a top table tennis player at school, Steve's careers adviser could only suggest banking or the civil service. So Steve ended up as a computer programmer/analyst in the Ministry of Defence and hung up his table tennis bat at the age of 25. He took up tennis as his serious hobby, and 5 years later took the plunge into a tennis coaching career, not recommended Steve adds, but somehow he survived.

Steve is married with two daughters and lives in Kent. He says that he is so grateful to his wife, also a tennis enthusiast, for her continual support with his tennis career.